Zen Meditation for Beginners

ZEN MEDITATION FOR BEGINNERS

A Practical Guide to Inner Calm

BONNIE MYOTAI TREACE

For general information on our other products and services or to obtain technical support, please contact our Customer Care Department within the United States at (866) 744-2665, or outside the United States at (510) 253-0500.

Rockridge Press publishes its books in a variety of electronic and print formats. Some content that appears in print may not be available in electronic books, and vice versa.

Interior and Cover Designer: Tricia Jang
Art Producer: Megan Baggott
Editor: Andrea Leptinsky

ISBN: Print 978-1-64739-089-1
eBook 978-1-64739-090-7

Ro

FOR MY
MEDITATION
TEACHERS

CONTENTS

Introduction X

Zen Meditation Basics 1

Principle 1: Now Is the Right Time 27

Principle 2: This Is the Right Place 39

Principle 3: You Are the Right One 51

Principle 4: Rest Your Gaze 63

Principle 5: You Are a Being of Compassion 75

Principle 6: Integrity Happens Now 87

Principle 7: Living from the Inside Out 99

Principle 8: Just Wash Your Bowls 109

Principle 9: Your Body Knows 121

Principle 10: Contentment amid Chaos 133

Resources 142

Index 144

THE GREAT PATH HAS NO GATES,
THOUSANDS OF ROADS ENTER IT.
WHEN ONE PASSES THROUGH THIS GATELESS GATE
ONE WALKS FREELY BETWEEN HEAVEN AND EARTH.

– ZEN MASTER MUMON (1183–1260)

INTRODUCTION

I like to tell this story: I began meditating when I was around seven years old. Like most stories, it is likely I have made a good deal of this up over the years, but I'm fond of the memory. I was lying in the grass under a tree in Omaha watching a cricket. I got down as close to it as I could and was spellbound—it was so completely still. Then with all of the drama a seven-year-old can muster, I promised myself I wouldn't move until it did.

What I remember is not moving for a very, very long time—hours and hours—and that the sun was beginning to go down when the cricket finally hopped away. But perhaps it was just a couple of minutes. The grass swayed a little with the breeze, but the cricket and I didn't budge. And at a certain

point there was a strange shift, like I had been working hard to be quiet and still, but then it didn't take any work at all. I was awake, but my worries were asleep. When the cricket suddenly leapt, everything jumped back to the way it was before, yet I was immensely content. I couldn't really say what had happened, but I'd found out something very important about how being still could change my perception and feelings.

Many of us have these experiences of natural meditation, which sometimes appear haphazardly yet show us a more relaxed and intentional way to inhabit our minds and participate in the world. We know there's the possibility, even though we can't necessarily summon it at will. The Zen tradition calls this "chasing a feather with a fan." The more you reach for the feather, the farther out of reach it becomes. For me, the question of what meditation actually was became a deep search. I knew it was "real," but the more I tried to understand and achieve it, the less accessible it seemed.

When I came across Zen Buddhism and its teachings on meditation, it spoke directly to the heart of my questions. I began to do *zazen*, or seated meditation, in my dorm room. I told my teacher that I was going to find a

place to study Zen and throw myself fully into whatever it entailed. (Yes, my early twenties were still as informed by dramatic proclamations as my childhood had been.)

After several years of meditating on my own, I entered a full-time residential Zen monastery in 1983. Twenty-plus years later, I had become a priest, been designated a Zen teacher (Sensei), and was the Vice-Abbot of my monastery. In addition, I had completed formal koan study with my teacher, continued study with several other teachers, and was the first "dharma successor" in my order. It was then that I established the Zen Center of New York City, which would serve as a spiritual home and practice center for thousands of people, and continues today as one of the most active Buddhist centers in the city. After several years, I left New York and started a nonresidential training program called Hermitage Heart, with students throughout the United States.

After studying with many wonderful teachers and thousands of students for almost forty years, I am very grateful for Zen—and I am committed to sharing it with whomever is interested. Teaching in New York City, I've worked with people from all social, cultural, and economic backgrounds. All of us face the issue of what it is to be human, to endure illness, to confront aging and death, and to weather the stressors of our time. I've sat together with patients in hospitals. I've taught in prisons. But no matter the setting or situation, breath by breath, Zen meditation practitioners find their implicit freedom and capacity for compassion and forgiveness (often for themselves).

For all of us, spiritual practice begins with a commitment to exploring the unknown. We have to decide to not settle for distracted lives or live on the sidelines of our own existence. One translation of Zen (全) means "whole" or "all." As we explore Zen, our challenge is to observe how that wholeness functions and how it works in our beautifully ordinary yet particular lives. We call this kind of meditation "the whole works"—as in, "Give me that pizza with the works." What we are embracing is a spiritual life that enables the full range of possibilities. But before we do that, we will get still and quiet, like a cricket on a leaf of grass.

What Is Zen Meditation?

Zen is the meditation school of Buddhism. It centers around the example of Siddhartha Guatama, known later as Shakyamuni Buddha, who sat down with his own heart and mind and came to peace. "Buddha" simply means the "one who awakens." Awakening, in this sense, points to realizing what is true—what the basic nature of being human really is. Several centuries ago in India, when Siddhartha became starkly aware of human suffering, old age, and death, he could not fathom how anyone lived at ease amid awareness of such sorrows. He studied with all the great teachers of his day, doing all of the practices they taught, and was still unresolved. One day, he decided that all that was left was to sit down and thoroughly and devotedly study his own heart and the coursing of his mind. After a long time and encountering many vexations, he did indeed awaken. Though he emphasized that what he had seen could not technically be taught or given from one person to another—rather, it could only be realized deep within the individual—his teaching still inspired many thousands of lives in many countries. The practice of sitting down and trusting the wholeness of one's own life, and seeing the interconnectedness of all things, is Zen meditation. That is what this book is about—not just understanding Buddhism as a religion, but actually practicing the heart of it with your own body and mind.

How to Use This Book

This book will equip you with what you need to get started with Zen meditation practice immediately. This is because practicing—taking up your own breath and life consciously—is really the only way to understand Zen, and yourself, with any clarity. Later, you may find some of the poetry and teachings helpful and supportive, but initially only one thing is required: to simply begin. This means sitting down in the center of your life, becoming still, and dropping the masks and defenses you use to defend the various ideas you have about yourself.

The practice of Zen takes place in the beauty and clarity of the present moment. This means releasing the habit of spiraling into the past and future. Zen has been called "the religion before religion," which is to say that anyone can practice it, even those committed to another faith. The phrase also points to the natural religion of our early childhood, when even the smallest thing—like a daisy plucked from the sidewalk—could open up an infinity of wonder. One of the paradoxes of Buddhist meditation is that it is the practice of intentionally working with your mind to return to, or awaken, what is most natural and uncontrived.

In the short course presented in these pages, you will encounter ten different principles of Zen practice. Each principle functions as a gateway into the oneness, or undivided reality, that touches all aspects of life.

Each chapter is structured the same way. First, I will put forth a principle and describe why you may find it helpful. Then, we'll look into some of the common obstacles encountered around that principle and how to work with them. This will be followed by one or two related exercises that demonstrate how to bring the principle to life, both on the meditation pillow and off.

We'll examine many questions on our meditation journey. For example: What is real commitment when the stakes are high but the steps are small? What is our responsibility when chaos and crises seem to be the state of things? Again and again, we will look for insight, consider our challenges, and introduce a beginner's practice of meditation with straightforward steps to continue on the path. The emphasis on small steps is intentional. The easiest way to overwhelm yourself with "the whole works" is to think of it as too demanding and too huge to encounter in your already-busy days.

So we'll start with a breath or two, for a minute or two, simply shifting our minds from distraction to the center. It's often said that we create our lives through what we give attention to. Every time we come home to that center, we recognize that it's always near. The more we practice, the easier it is to see—this truth, this still center, is available whenever we choose to give it our undivided attention.

Zen Meditation Basics

Most of us wander for many years, seeking to address the quiet but inescapable longing to be at home in our lives. Perhaps we read a bit of spiritual teaching or hear a stray comment from a friend who practices meditation, and somehow the vague outline of a path homeward begins to reveal itself.

We may not be able to articulate what we're seeking, only that we can't ignore the call within ourselves. A priority becomes clear: to find what is most important and live in terms of it. In one sense, Zen arrives in that moment. It is a way of seeing clearly the nature of the self and a way of living based on that clarity.

Still, the truth is that distractions are part of life. Work, family, health, creativity, and being a responsible citizen all fill our hours to the brim. When we first encounter the tradition of Zen, it can seem overwhelming. You might wonder how on earth a meditation practice can fit into your already-full life. Indeed, it can be unclear how the poetry of Zen Buddhism (and the sometimes confusing literature surrounding it) can have anything to do with our daily lives.

Because of this, it's important to start slowly, to cull through the myths around Zen meditation and find the small inroads into a fulfilling practice. That's what this book is for. Its aim is to provide information (and inspiration) that will help you get a meditation practice planted in your life. We'll work the soil and soften the resistance. We'll concentrate particularly on seated meditation, though we'll explore how each posture and activity of human life can become a place of practice.

The emphasis in these pages will be to engage and actually practice. That is how you create a crack in the ego's armor, allowing the light in. The practice will grow naturally from there, and we'll weed the path that tends to get overgrown with ideas and preconceptions, opinions and abstractions. Our work is to keep returning to the doing—the actualizing—so that we're bringing the freshness of life to each moment.

Zen Buddhism: The Beginning of the Meditative Tradition

Meditation is a way to address and clarify how distorted our perceptions usually are. In fact, when the original Buddha first awakened to his true nature, his comment was that it was absolutely amazing and that every single being had exactly the same wisdom and capacity for compassion as the most Enlightened One did. So why didn't all beings live from this truth? The answer lies in those distorted perceptions. We live with tremendous problems that arise because of our habitual, dualistic way of thinking, but deep down we are perfect and capable of discernment and unconditional, loving action.

The meditation at the heart of the Zen tradition of Buddhism is an expression of the "nondual." It is an invitation to step out of the huge bias we tend to have in how we see the world. Most of us habitually split the world into categories without much reflection: good and bad, ordinary and sacred, us and them. And we then run our world from these biases. But it's not that logical thinking and analysis are bad—they're usually the best method if we're designing a building, doing accounting, or any number of other projects. The issue is that it's not useful for us to think only analytically when discerning the nondual. What does this mean, exactly? Our culture conditions us to value the rational and logical and to devalue our direct experience. As a result, we separate from ourselves and step back to look at things, rather than stepping into each moment and simply being. From that separation flows loneliness, longing, frustration, and distraction.

Among the various Buddhist traditions, the Zen school uses meditation as its central practice. Zen doesn't require worship, belief in doctrines, or devotion. It isn't theistic, meaning based on the existence of a god. But it's not atheistic or agnostic either. It neither proposes nor denies God—it simply doesn't take up the question of God as necessary to spiritual practice. The historic Buddha is understood as an ordinary human being who freed himself from dissatisfaction (in Sanskrit: *dukkha*) and then taught others about the possibility of doing the same. For the 2,600 years since this enlightenment, practitioners of all genders, lay and monastic, old and young, have taken up this possibility in their own lives, experiencing the freedom at the heart of the tradition.

BUDDHA'S TEACHINGS

As we noted earlier, Zen traces itself back to Siddhartha Guatama, who came to be known as Shakyamuni Buddha. Let's dive into that story a little deeper. Born more than 2,600 years ago into a royal family in present-day Nepal, Siddhartha led a very sheltered and privileged life until one day he traveled outside the gates of his palace. In this moment, all of his assumptions about life were fundamentally disrupted by several stark realities: He saw someone suffering with sickness, someone diminished by aging, and someone who had died. He also saw a holy man, someone who engaged in spiritual practices. All of this was new to his awareness and shook him of the innocence and indulgence that, up until then, had seemed natural. He was so shocked, in fact, that he left his compound altogether and began an intense path of self-exploration and study. He gave away all his belongings, shaved his head, and put on simple robes. He lived in utmost simplicity and sought out the great and respected teachers of his day, looking for a way to be genuinely at peace.

Now, let's bring it back to the present day for a moment. We can think of Siddhartha as the ancient archetype for the modern seeker who starts a spiritual search in earnest and goes from retreat center to retreat center, self-help book to self-help book, seeking answers, teachers, and methods. The ideas and patterns that once satisfied them are no longer enough. We leave behind the things that once seemed to offer protection, or a sense of definition, and begin the journey toward greater maturity. But it takes time for us to find our way.

Despite his earnest seeking, nothing Siddhartha learned fully addressed his deepest questions. What was life really about? Why was there so much suffering? Were we here "for" anything? Even though he'd diligently taken up every practice—extreme fasting, stepping away from pleasures, keen intellectual inquiry—nothing brought him the peace he sought. Every state he would accomplish was temporary. Eventually, he decided that the path of deprivation wasn't effective. After becoming emaciated, he took a different tack and began nourishing his body, regained his strength, and decided that the only thing left to do was to look directly into his own mind. And for six years, he did simply that. He sat under a favorite tree remembered from his childhood, often for long periods without moving, gazing into the depths of his own consciousness. Finally, he knew he was close to closing the gap between himself and the truth he sought. In that ripeness, he promised himself not to get up until his questions were resolved.

Many days and nights passed as he sat in quiet contemplation. Then, one night, as he saw the morning star, he reached *anuttara samyak sambhodi*—great and perfect enlightenment. This is described in various ways in various texts, but all somewhat inadequately. You can say he "touched the ground of being," that "the separate self fell away," that "the eye that cannot see itself was realized." But all descriptions miss the essentially intimate nature of enlightenment. His teachings for the rest of his life, and Buddhism for centuries to come, directly evoked that profound intimacy with all things.

THE FOUR NOBLE TRUTHS

Witnessing his transformation, the Buddha's fellow monks begged him to teach them what he had come to understand. Being asked by such heartfelt companions, the Buddha was called to begin the impossible task of "teaching what cannot be taught."

His first teaching began with acknowledging *dukkha*, or "suffering." He explained that because everything was changing all the time, humans tend to always be striving and grasping. Impermanence itself created a state of discontent. Even if we have what we want, we know things can change—in fact, we know they will. And so there is a constant murmur in the human heart of discontent. This shared, and seemingly inescapable, dissatisfaction is what helped formed the basis of what he called the Four Noble Truths:

1. **LIFE SUFFERS DIS-EASE.** We are aware of impermanence and so cannot settle into peace.

2. **THIS SUFFERING HAS A CAUSE, A BEGINNING.** The Buddha identified that our idea that we are essentially separate from others is the beginning, the source, of ongoing dissatisfaction.

3. **IT IS POSSIBLE TO END THIS SUFFERING.** Whatever has a beginning has an end. Our suffering begins with an idea, and though hard to imagine, it is possible to live without that idea.

4. **THERE IS A WAY TO DO SO.** This is the life of practice that the Buddha called The Eightfold Path.

The Buddha wasn't being negative by emphasizing suffering and dissatisfaction in his first offering. He, like a good doctor, was starting with an accurate diagnosis of the human condition. Then, having the patient's attention, he offered medicine. He modeled the truth that if we try to skip over our pain, we limit our ability to feel true contentment. Being still and resting in direct experience, regardless of its contents, is what allows contentment to find us. Only then can things shift. He said, "Both in the past, and now, I have set forth only this: dukkha and the end of dukkha."

THE EIGHTFOLD PATH

The eight aspects of the path to liberation from suffering are grouped into three essential elements of Buddhist practice: moral conduct, mental discipline, and wisdom. The Buddha taught the Noble Eightfold Path in virtually all his discourses. In one sense, what it points to is that every part of our life matters—what we do, say, and think are each critical to spiritual life. In most translations, the elements of the Eightfold Path each begin with the word *right*. It is important to understand that this is not right as opposed to wrong, but rather indicative of completeness and centeredness, akin to "righting" a ship that is off-kilter.

THE NOBLE EIGHTFOLD PATH

1. **RIGHT UNDERSTANDING**
2. **RIGHT THOUGHT**
3. **RIGHT SPEECH**
4. **RIGHT ACTION**
5. **RIGHT LIVELIHOOD**
6. **RIGHT EFFORT**
7. **RIGHT MINDFULNESS**
8. **RIGHT CONCENTRATION**

Practically the whole teaching of the Buddha, which lasted forty-five years, deals in some way or other with this path. He explained it in different ways and in different words to different people, according to the stage of their development and their capacity to understand. But the essence of those many thousand discourses scattered in the Buddhist scriptures is found in the Noble Eightfold Path.

The eight categories, or divisions, of the path are not to be followed and practiced one after the other, but are to be developed more or less simultaneously. They are all linked together; each supports the cultivation of the others. The eight elements aim at promoting and perfecting the three essentials of Buddhist training and discipline: ethical conduct (*sila*), mental discipline (*samadhi*), and wisdom (*panna*).

Zen Meditation in Daily Life

The Buddha taught that there were four postures for meditation: sitting down, standing up, lying down, and walking. This was his way of indicating that every position and activity of our lives can be a place of meditation.

Of course, we'll face some common challenges in our meditation journey. We might feel like there is no time available to meditate. And when we do meditate, it might make us more honest about our state of mind, which isn't always convenient or comfortable. Our knees or neck might ache now and then. Or we'll sit down and find that everything else is suddenly more interesting than just breathing and being in our Buddha nature. As soon as we sit down to quiet the mind, we'll remember the dry cleaning or the groceries we forgot to get.

I liken meditation to training a puppy. Patience, persistence, and gentleness change a wayward puppy into a stellar companion. Our mind is just like that—all over the place, full of random and intense emotions, making a mess of life's carpet. And then we give time and space to let it settle into itself, and we become our own best companion. This is the simple challenge of meditation: We have to show up for it and give it our attention and faith. When we do that consistently, working with and through the frustrations, the drama gradually calms down, and we are home.

INTERRUPTION SCIENCE

There's a phrase from one of my talks that a student told me she copied onto a slip of paper and revisits when she's feeling frazzled:

There is no interruption. There is only This, letting go of This. And then there is This.

Once you get interrupted, it can take a really long time to get back to what you're doing. It can take several minutes, sometimes even a half hour, to get fully engaged again with our original task. Our brains are predisposed toward distraction, and those who sit in front of a computer—an endless source of novelty—typically work for only 40 seconds before being distracted or interrupted.

According to an interesting brain imaging study at Emory University School of Medicine, experienced Zen meditators often can clear their minds of distractions more quickly than novices. The study found that after being interrupted by a task, the brains of experienced meditators returned faster to their conditions before the interruption. While it's not exactly the best or only reason to meditate, it's a definite benefit to practicing. Meditation helps us limit the influence that distracting thoughts will have on us.

TIME AND MEDITATION

When we meditate, the question of time arises. We have to decide when to meditate, how long to meditate, and how to integrate meditation into the rest of our day. Is there a best time? The tradition of Zen has usually identified early mornings and late evenings as the most fruitful times.

Time itself can seem less "regular." Sometimes meditating for five minutes will feel like an hour, and sometimes an hour can pass and will seem like no time at all.

Morning is beneficial because the agenda of the day hasn't begun yet. A morning meditation can set us sailing into our busy lives with deeper intention and greater calm. Most home meditators find that morning meditation can be built into the day with just a slightly earlier wake-up. Before bed is also good because it relaxes the body for sleep and helps us let go of anything we are carrying around from the day. See if you can fit in a short meditation as part of your getting-ready-for-bed routine; you'll likely find it the opposite of another thing on the to-do list.

When you first start a meditation practice, it's usually counterproductive—and unrealistic—to set a huge time commitment for yourself, such as meditating for an hour every morning and night. While you may have the best intentions, it's hard to stick to such an ambitious goal—and within a short while, it falls off the schedule.

When students ask me how long to meditate, I often say, "Just let your butt hit the pillow every day." Even if you just sit down for a second, the very gesture of showing up will have an impact. I've heard from many students over the years that this is the instruction that helped them most. Otherwise they'd talk themselves out of meditation by saying that they're too tired or they've forgotten why they even wanted to start meditating. Simply showing up for a very brief moment made all the difference.

That's the spirit of this book. The practices you'll find here take almost no time at all. I encourage you to make the commitment to go through each of the principles and their bite-size approach. I think you'll find that when there is a natural draw within you to practice, your life will reorganize with the time to do it.

You may find yourself sitting for a half hour one morning or an hour on a Saturday afternoon not as a big act of discipline, but because it feels right. With practice, even when you encounter an obstacle, you will find it is not something that throws you off your pillow.

I remember going through a period when all I had to do was sit down for meditation and it would feel like I hadn't slept for ages and I'd become completely groggy. As I "sat through" the grogginess, it was as if a whole new relationship to meditation took shape. It was no longer about feeling any particular way and much more about trusting that every experience and state is worth showing up for. So with that in mind, please take these small bites and trust yourself to find your way into a life of meditation.

Zen Meditation in Practice

You might have heard of zazen as the typical form of Zen meditation. But what is zazen?

There are many techniques and traditions when it comes to meditation. Some involve introducing a focus, an object, a mantra, and placing the mind "there." Other meditations you'll encounter under the banner of mindfulness.

Zazen literally means "seated Zen." It's more stripped down in the sense that it asks that we stop introducing ideas, such as where the mind should be focused, and allows the mind to simply be. It also recognizes that focus is not necessarily always a "good" thing in meditation. We can, after all, focus on anything, including very negative or selfish things. The tradition of zazen brings into play the nature of the self and a deep understanding of interconnectedness, which naturally evoke a life of compassionate activity.

We tend to come to meditation with all sorts of ideas about what it is supposed to be. Maybe the image of the Buddha beneath the Bodhi Tree is in our head. Or perhaps it's a wise robed monk in the hilltops. But zazen is never in the image—it exists only as a practice. Whatever we think about it separates it from us. The key is to drop all the things we think meditation or zazen should be and find ourselves simply sitting.

You may have heard this startling expression: "If you meet the Buddha on the road, kill him." What does this mean? It's referencing this concept of not putting the Buddha outside yourself. Kill the idea of what the Buddha should be and simply *be* the Buddha practicing.

It's very easy to say "just sit." Of course, doing it can be much more challenging. Even in the moments we actually do sit without an intervening idea, it's easy to follow with the thought, "That was it! I was actually doing zazen!" And with that, we've separated ourselves from the utter intimacy of meditation. Zazen is really just that.

PREPARING YOUR SPACE

My teacher used to say, "The best place to meditate is wherever you find yourself." In other words, don't wait to find some perfect place, or you'll never get started. Let this be the place and time. Enter it "shoes off," without protecting yourself, and set down your heavy backpack of ideas and excuses. Decide to begin.

It can be helpful to designate a certain place in your home where you will practice. Put a chair or the cushion you use for seated meditation in a corner of a room. Consider creating an altar to remind yourself that life is sacred. Use any small table and arrange on it a candle, a bowl to offer incense, some fresh flowers in a vase, and maybe a picture of a teacher or other supportive figure in your life. When you see this space, it will serve as a physical reminder of your commitment to meditate. If you share space, setting up a designated meditation space lets your housemates know this is a real priority in your life.

Your designated meditation space also serves as a way of inviting yourself into practice; it is like an open doorway into your deeper intentions. Be a gracious and skillful host for your tender practice. Even if you sit for only five minutes (or one), let it be a physical expression of your impulse toward clarity and love. You are here to be refreshed. You are in the good company of all who commit to a conscious, compassionate life. With my students who have mobility issues or use assistive devices, sometimes we find a special shawl or cloth that creates the space when they shift toward meditation. As that cloth gets spread or the shawl brought around their shoulders, they bring to the room a certain kindness that invites their commitment.

When you're away from home, creating space becomes more subtle than a familiar pillow in front of an altar. Again, having some physical cues are helpful. Some students use a "portable altar" or simply a candle (even a battery-powered tea candle) to help shift their consciousness toward meditation while in a hotel or guest room.

Even more subtle is the meditation that uses whichever space you are in as the cue. With my New York City students, for instance, we had a special practice whenever we entered an elevator, to let the closing of the door be the creation of a "tiny temple." We held whomever else was in the elevator-temple in our heart as a teacher, and the ping as each floor ticked by was a little wake-up bell. (We also tried this with subway rides, although everyone found this a much more advanced practice!)

PREPARING YOUR BODY

If you look at pictures of Zen meditation, you'll likely notice that most people use two pillows: a small round pillow called a *zafu* and a larger flat square of a pillow called a *zabuton*. The zafu rests on the zabuton. When you sit cross-legged on the front third of the zafu, which is 4 to 5 inches tall, your legs will naturally incline to the floor. It's helpful to get at least one knee to the ground for stability. For those who are flexible enough to sit on the floor, there is a bit of added relaxation just from being close to the ground. (Some think it has something to do with the mind releasing any tension around falling.)

One popular position is called a "full lotus." Here, you form a perfect tripod by having each foot rest on its opposite thigh. With stretching, and time, many (especially young) people can do this very stable position. There's also the "half lotus," which has just one foot on the opposite thigh—this is slightly less stable, but also quite fine. In my experience, most people sit in a position called "Burmese." This is cross-legged with one foot in front of the other on the floor. It's important in Burmese not to tuck one foot under the other, otherwise the bottom foot soon goes to sleep (and the drama of the sleeping foot ensues).

FULL LOTUS HALF LOTUS BURMESE

Another option is kneeling, either by sitting sideways on a zafu to take pressure off the ankles, or by using a kneeling bench, called a *seiza bench*, for the same purpose. And, of course, you can also meditate simply sitting in a chair. The key to comfort and balance with all these positions is to have the bottom slightly higher than the knees. In a chair, try not to lean against the back while putting both feet flat on the floor. If you lean against the back of the chair, you eliminate the natural curve in your lower spine that provides good support. Take notice if a kind of spiritual pride pushes you to take a posture that's too much for your body. In other words, if you've injured your knee, please sit in a chair.

The idea is to sit with an erect and upright posture that supports attention. After figuring out what you're doing with your legs, either on a pillow or chair, elongate the spine for a moment and then relax, allowing the natural curve in the lower back. In other words, don't sit "soldier straight," but do use the real support of your back doing what it does best. It can help to briefly sway from side to side so that your spine centers over the torso and tightness releases from the hips. For those doing bed or wheelchair meditation, a pillow prop that helps align the back can be helpful. Some of my students like a 2-to-3-foot cylinder-style pillow, like the ones used in restorative yoga, positioning it upright from the base of the chair.

Tuck the chin in slightly, without leaning the head forward. Place your hands in your lap, with your less dominant hand resting atop your more active hand, allowing the thumbs to touch lightly, creating an oval. This is called the "cosmic mudra," which will act as a built-in biofeedback device, letting you know whether your mind is wandering or holding stress. How? If your thumbs drift apart, your mind is wandering. If they press hard against one another, you are holding tension. And if they come to rest in your palm rather than forming the oval, you're likely drifting into sleep.

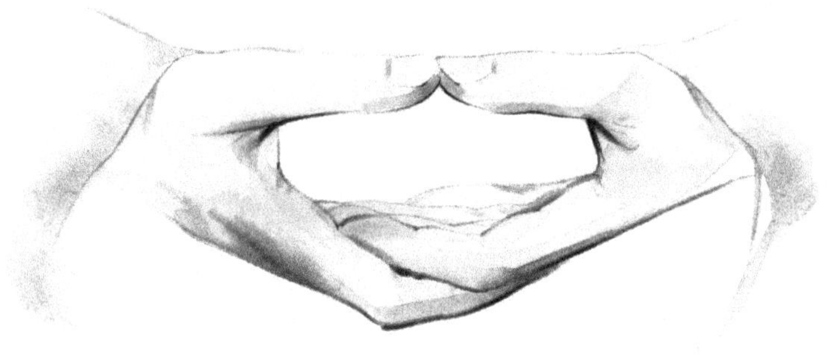

COSMIC MUDRA

Let your elbows rest slightly away from the body, which will also release shoulder tension. In Zen meditation, we sit with the eyes slightly open, letting the gaze rest softly a few feet ahead. It can help to press the tongue lightly against the upper palate, relaxing the jaw muscles. Once you've created the body posture, you'll begin to work with the breath.

The Power of Breath

The power of our breath in meditation is called *ki*, which means "life force." When we are first settling to meditation, the breath is sometimes used as an object of concentration, a way of meditating with and through the body, not just with the mind or the intellect. We are asked to trust the breath "as it is" without elongating or deepening it, but just resting our awareness in it as it flows naturally. This simple gesture of attention to a thing, without altering or "fixing" it, also opens the door to understanding how meditation will teach us about the world—not by changing it, but by "being it" and not separating ourselves from any one thing, person, or condition. This is a very powerful transition for many of us, and shifts us from encountering life as a problem to be solved to a simple and radical presence.

New meditators will be taught to use their inhales and exhales to count up to ten and then begin again at one, continuing to count with each movement of the breath again and again up to the number ten. If the mind wanders along the way, we acknowledge that, and then resume counting, but beginning again with the number one. Sometimes, when the mind is very distracted, a meditator may only count "one . . . two" and then begin chasing a thought. Eventually, concentration does deepen, and the counting is no longer necessary. You simply place awareness on the breath itself; the instruction is to just "be the breath." In later forms of meditation, even this focus on the breath is released.

PREPARING YOUR MIND

Zen has no gates. The purpose of Buddha's words is to enlighten others. Therefore Zen should be gateless. Now, how does one pass through this gateless gate? Some say that whatever enters through a gate is not family treasure, that whatever is produced by the help of another is likely to dissolve and perish. Even such words are like raising waves in a windless sea or performing an operation upon a healthy body.

—Master Mumon, 12th-century Chinese Zen Master

As Master Mumon indicates, Zen is not out to make you better; you are whole and perfect from the beginning. You are already where you need to be. The "family treasure" is your very life; you don't need an outside expert to tell you its truth. To simply believe what someone else has said elsewhere is called "putting another head on top of your own." Zen meditation and the practices it includes become relevant and real only as they are tested in your own body and mind. Don't believe the Buddha, or me, or any teacher. Just practice and see for yourself.

The following ten principles of Zen will consist of words of inspiration and insight, common obstacles, and ways to practice each of the areas. It is a short course that's specifically designed to fit into busy lives. Yet it is "the whole works" in that it will also invite you to explore every idea and presumption. It is, as Mumon said, all about *not* missing the chance to realize your implicit freedom.

SETTING YOUR INTENTION

I offer the following intention to bring with you as you enter your Zen meditation practice.

In the Zen tradition, intentions are often framed as vows, with wording that has been passed down for many centuries. But the spirit of making a vow is that we fold the past, present, and future into a single, powerful possibility. An intention or vow is a thorough dedication of your energy—of thoughts, words, and deeds—toward creating the clearest and most compassionate reality.

You may embrace these intentions or develop your own.

May we be a force for good in the world.
May we rest in the present, realizing the clarity and beauty of each moment.
May we take off the armor of ego, stop creating hollow longings one after another, and find peace in the home of our heart and mind.

PRINCIPLE 1

Now Is the Right Time

No matter what mistakes we make, we can start over because everything is impermanent. We can change. We can change the direction of our life.

—Shohaku Okumura, Soto Zen Priest

Meditation is moment by moment. As an old teacher of mine used to remind us, "If you miss the moment, you miss your life." But how do we come to the moment, fresh and awake to all its potential, without dragging along the past nor being distracted by ideas about the future? To begin, we have to let go. Let go of what? Everything but the bare, perfect moment, without our ideas piled on top of it. To meditate is to let go. To put it another way: To meditate is to not hold on.

There is an alternative to the exhausting and vain attempt to hold on amid the vitally coursing stream of consciousness. During meditation we often say, "You can't stop the river, but you can choose not to build a house on whatever log is floating by." It may even feel like your mind is actually busier—there are so many thoughts! The key, again, is to not get hooked by any of them. Stay present with the river itself, if you will, and don't worry about or judge what may float downstream.

In Zen meditation, we practice this noticing and letting go. That's it, moment by moment. There is no "bad" moment to meditate. As your mind begins to recognize this, it will relax its grip and become more open. There's an energy release when the dynamics of avoidance and labor are dissolved. When we stop trying to hold on to states of mind or certain life conditions,

we can begin to find peace in the fact that everything changes. Ideas and ideals, fears and regrets, will constantly arise. Breathe. Notice. Relax. And when you can, Let Go. None of these constructs are who you are, so don't build a dwelling out of any of them and pretend you can make your home there. Let your grip relax. Holding on has never worked. With a little attention, you'll notice your true home arriving every moment.

Return the Heart to Daybreak

One of the greatest gifts of meditation is that it always gives us a second chance (or even perpetual chances). It is always a beginning, returning the heart to daybreak. Meditation is letting go of the idea that we have a fixed identity that precludes all other possibilities. It is letting go of both enlightened thoughts and deluded thoughts.

Without denying *karma*—the force of an action to continue in a given direction—Zen meditation delivers us home to the moment, where we can start fresh. As we rest in the present moment, we regain the freedom we too often forget we have: to act in accordance with what is, and what is possible, rather than the constrictions of our conditioning. Every moment contains the past and the future, everything that has ever been or might ever be. That is the breath taken in meditation. It creates a kind of resilient tenderness to stand at that daybreak threshold, responsible and capable. All of the pain and confusion, the mistakes and the victories, are present. But for now, you can stop telling their stories. You don't have to prove anything. The time has come to simply trust yourself.

LET GO OF YESTERDAY

Will Rogers, the American cowboy humorist, once said, "Don't let yesterday use too much of today." Perhaps the hardest thing when we start meditation is to believe that we don't need any of yesterday's ideas. We don't have to keep repeating the inner lists or succumb to our drama. We don't need to prove we're good enough.

Zen meditation involves "emptying the mind" in the sense that we are letting both small thoughts and important realizations pass. Yet most of us will try to hold on to whatever is nagging us from yesterday, or even years past. Even when it's not making us happy, or doesn't feel particularly true, we'll return to our pattern. It takes time in the quiet and stillness of meditation to trust yourself.

Be willing to keep returning, noticing the thoughts and ideas, the anxieties and grand schemes. Eventually, some space will open up between the thoughts. You'll slowly begin to find that spaciousness more and more interesting; the chatter, a little less so. The option to identify with that spaciousness, rather than the come-and-go thoughts, will become more available. And when you shift your interest to awareness, everything shifts.

AWARENESS OF BREATH

How do you begin with your Zen meditation practice? As infuriating as it might sound, the answer is: just start. Sit down, settle your posture (see the Zen Meditation Basics section on page 1 if you need a refresher), get into a good relationship with gravity, lower your gaze, and connect to your breath.

Make a commitment to spend an allotted amount of time giving your full attention to the sensation of breathing. It could be as little as four breaths in and four breaths out. When thoughts arise, acknowledge them, then consciously and deliberately let them go, returning the attention to the breath.

Don't make the breath deeper, elongate it, or otherwise mess with it in any way. Simply give it your attention. Think of it as becoming a friend to your breath. Accept that sometimes it is deep and sometimes it is shallow. Don't judge it—just be with it, attentively. Most people begin to be aware of how the breath makes the belly rise a little on the inhale and go down with the exhale. There may be a breath or two that gets tighter, reacting to attention with a self-conscious awkwardness. That will calm down as you allow the breath to be itself.

As with anything we give attention to, it will likely become deeper as time goes on, but wherever you start is exactly where you need to be. Obviously, and importantly meditating is not just about sitting cross-legged. As you practice your breath, you are practicing a way of being that goes wherever you breathe. And so, now let's move through the first meditation.

HOW DO I KNOW IF I'M "IN" MEDITATION?

There are few things I can predict when I give meditation instruction to a group. One thing that always comes up during the question-and-answer period is some variation of "I think I did it wrong." Or "I'm not sure if I meditated or just sat here thinking the whole time." It's normal to want to know if we're doing it right—we don't want to waste time or spin uselessly around in our heads. But the truth is: There is no "doing it wrong."

This mind you are befriending in meditation is a chatty and wily character. It is both insecure and arrogant. It will want constant reassurance and, at seemingly the same time, be convinced it has seen eternal truths. To be its friend, try not to judge it. But don't buy into its drama either. The need to know whether you're doing meditation right, whether you are "in" meditation, is the mind's anxiety, craving assurance. It is part of our habit of leaving intimate experience and objectifying our lives.

The antidote to this question is to just begin, again and again. Notice the thought, let it go, and come back to the breath. The thought may be "Now I'm doing it!" Or "What am I doing?" Or "I'm not doing anything!" Give your attention to the thought, and when you can, let it pass and head downriver with all the others. Here's your breath waiting for you. Inhale, exhale . . . just begin.

MEDITATION

5 MINUTES

DAYSTART

When you plan to meditate in the morning, do your best the night before to get a good night's sleep. On waking, it's fine to have a quick cup of coffee or tea if you need to, but avoid turning on your computer or engaging in social media. While a morning meditation may initially seem like a big drag (you're likely still a little sleepy), the benefit is that your mind hasn't had a chance to fully plug in to the agenda of the day. As a result, your thoughts won't be as aggressive. Mornings are also a time when our appreciation of having that new start—that second chance—is possibly most clear.

1. Approach the place you will meditate and make a small standing bow.
2. Set a timer for five minutes. It can help to offer a stick of incense, but the only necessary "prop" is you.
3. Take your meditation position in a chair or on a floor pillow.
4. Lower your gaze and bring your attention to your breath. Don't try to change the breath—just let yourself feel it. Where do you feel it in your body? How do you experience it moving? Notice if your nostrils feel a little cool when you inhale, or if you can sense that slight expansion in your

belly right before the exhale begins. Your breath is going to help you develop concentration, so give yourself over to it for these five minutes.

5. When other thoughts come up—and they will—acknowledge them. Do your best to catch them before they develop too extensively. Whenever you do notice them, consciously and deliberately let them go, and then bring your attention back to the sensation of your breathing.

There are, of course, all variety of thoughts and emotions that may arise. Your meditation is not to suppress any of them but simply to develop the capacity to put your attention where you need it, for as long as you need it there. Trust that if something comes up during meditation that you need to deal with in your life, that thought will return at its appropriate time. For now, really get to know your breath.

Some of us will encounter residual sleepiness, either in the daystart meditation period or at night, when we're tired from the day. Again, like any state, there is nothing wrong with this. If you find yourself nodding off, notice it, and let yourself have a nice inhale, inviting a more alert attention. Be caring with yourself—we all go through times when meditation is closer to a nap than a great awakening of any sort. The key? Just show up for your commitment of five minutes and experience your practice. The tendency toward sleepiness, like everything, will change. One day it will have passed, and you will have "a new something" to let go!

MEDITATION

3 MINUTES

Water Blessing

As you encounter water for the first time after waking (splashing your face, taking a drink), take a moment or two to consider water itself as a teacher. We are largely made of it, depend on it for life, and also bear the responsibility of keeping water safe for generations to come. It is both ordinary and extraordinary. This meditation is a very simple one that doesn't require you to sit in a particular place.

1. Set a timer for three minutes.
2. Copy the following lines (or memorize them) to recite to yourself each morning when you first run water from the tap:

   - Ordinary water
   - One taste
   - One life
   - This ordinary tap water
   - Impossible to earn.

This is one of the verses from *The Seven Thresholds of Zen*—a set of periodic "stopping exercises" (or *gathas*) I give my students. Let this first experience of water each day awaken your gratitude, interconnectedness, and awareness of a sacred obligation to all life.

POST-MEDITATION EXERCISE

The Whole Works

When the timer signals your meditation period is over, bring your hands together and make a small bow. Transitions matter and are a moment we often drop the thread. When we make them conscious, what we're doing on the pillow isn't a separate and isolated activity, but one part of a life being practiced. Try ending your morning meditation with the "Verse of the Buddha's Robe":

Vast is the robe of liberation
A formless field of benefaction
I wear the Tathagata's teaching
Saving all sentient beings.

It is a beautiful chant, though its meaning may not be immediately clear. The "Tathagata" is one who is "beyond coming and going," or all transitory phenomena. So, to wear the Tathagata's teaching is to live a life based in "the whole works"—non-dual, intimate, benefitting all beings. This saves beings by encountering them not as other, but as part of oneself, realizing that everyone and everything is not apart from the "formless field of benefaction."

In your home practice, this chant can be helpful. Try copying the words to the "Verse of the Buddha's Robe" and keep them visible to inspire and ground you. Before you leave morning meditation, feel free to say them to yourself one to three times.

PRINCIPLE 2

This Is the Right Place

The entire cosmos is a cooperative. The sun, the moon, and the stars live together as a cooperative. The same is true for humans and animals, trees, and the Earth. When we realize that the world is a mutual, interdependent, cooperative enterprise—then we can build a noble environment. If our lives are not based on this truth, then we shall perish.

—Buddhadasa Bhikkhu, 20th-century Thai ascetic-philosopher

It is perhaps Buddhism's most iconic image: Buddha in meditation, his left palm upright on his lap and his right hand reaching down and gently touching the Earth. In the storytelling part of Buddhist mythology, this image depicts a victorious moment. Evil forces have been trying everything to unseat the Buddha because the king of demons, Mara, wants the space under the Bodhi Tree for his own purposes. Mara demands that a witness be produced who can verify that the Buddha has had the spiritual awakening that would justify his being there.

This is when, without any hesitation, the Buddha extends his hand and simply touches the Earth. The Earth itself immediately responds, "I am your witness," and, voilà, Mara and his minions vanish. In this Earth-witness *mudra* (hand position), we celebrate the codependence of self and space, and of the meditator and environment.

Supported by the Earth

One of the things the story illustrates is that each of us are in exactly the right location to practice—and our practice is ineffably supported by (and supports) the whole Earth.

Practiced and realized in this way, meditation creates the "noble environment" of wisdom and compassion. But what is it to practice trusting that where we find ourselves is, indeed, the right place? What is it to understand in our cells that we are, in ways particular and general, responsible not just for the life inside the "skin bag" we call our self, but the whole catastrophe?

The Buddha began by just reaching down. Hand and Earth touch and witness one another. In a certain sense, that's where we all need to begin. The place we live, the land we occupy, the water we drink, and the air we breathe are all tied to our own body and mind. When the Earth suffers, we suffer. When the Earth is beloved, so are each one of us.

WHAT YOU NEED IS ALREADY HERE

Everyone knows how easy it is to blame geography, circumstance, and lifestyle for our problems. The much-derided "geographic cure" speaks to how frequently, if mistakenly, we think moving to a different situation will fix whatever is ailing us. The problem is that we take the problems with us;

where we go, they go. This is the best argument for actually sitting still in meditation. You directly face the quiet belief that if you just adjust your foot, or scratch your itchy nose, you'll settle into the right position to sit still, center yourself, breathe, and be clear and kind.

The truth is, moving to find the "better spot" is a fruitless journey. We never get there. Adjust your foot, and then your hip hurts. Scratch your nose, and suddenly your elbow itches. The search for perfect comfort can be endless. Until the moment we stop chasing something better. Until we recognize, and practice, the fact that the condition we need is not somewhere else. It takes a while to trust this, but it can completely change how a person deals with discomfort throughout their life. It's not that you never move, but that the fidgety, anxiety-driven chase for something we think might be better settles down.

So, the first challenge is to simply *stay*. All sorts of ideas will no doubt come and go: the city rat will dream of small-town bliss, while the country mouse will dream of the vibrance and vitality of urban life. Lay people might think becoming a monk or nun would be more spiritually supportive, while monastics will wonder if they're artificially protected from the realities of the human project and should get back out into the "real world." The obstacle in each case is the familiar grass-is-greener dream. The key is to not ditch the deep and sustaining ground we are on in favor of the vapor of a dream.

DEVELOPING CONCENTRATION

There are many "skillful means" (*upaya*) in the tradition of Zen that assist in developing concentration and attention. The various hand positions are among these skillful means. In addition to the Earth-witness mudra previously discussed (page 40), there are positions that help stabilize seated meditation. As we become less vulnerable to our impulses to find a different position or location, we are increasingly present where we are, both on and off the pillow. So, as mundane—or silly—as it may seem at first to place your hands in a particular position while meditating, it can actually have a huge impact on how you experience your life. As your meditation becomes steady, your life tends to become steady as well. And when your life is steadier, you're better able to see what's around and who or what needs you, and to be generous in how you serve.

The hand position most practitioners use is called the cosmic mudra (page 21), which creates what is supposed to be a circle, but may actually look a little more like an oval. The shape of this mudra symbolizes the completeness of the universe, which is both a central theme to Zen Buddhist teachings and a way of expressing the "noble environment" where nothing is missing. Of course, having a set hand position that you'll use in meditation also solves the age-old question of "What do I do with my hands?"

MEDITATION

5 MINUTES

Embodying Kindness

This meditation uses the cosmic mudra to assist your attention. The mudra is formed by cradling your dominant hand underneath your other hand, knuckles overlapping, with both palms facing up. You then bring the tips of your two thumbs gently together to make an oval, near-circular shape.

1. Take your meditation position in a chair or on the floor, set your timer, and lower your gaze.
2. Place your hands in your lap, resting the cosmic mudra against your belly, about two inches below the navel. This is the location of what Zen calls the *hara*, and it is the body's center of gravity. Bringing attention to the hara by placing the mudra there is literally centering.
3. Give your attention to the feeling of breathing, letting go of thoughts as they arise, and returning again and again to the breath and your hara.

4. If you notice during the period that your thumbs drift apart, bring them back together. Often, we'll notice the thumbs drifting before we actually notice our mind is drifting.

5. If you find your thumbs pressing hard one against the other, just lighten up and bring them back together easily. Let the thumbs touch with the pressure you would use to caress a child's face.

Many people find this albeit small practice of re-establishing the mudra to be the subtle launch of a new way of being with oneself, embodying a kindness we may have forgotten for too long a while.

MEDITATION

5 MINUTES

Handle with Care

We pick things up, move things from place to place, touch surfaces, and rub our tired eyes—our hands are a huge part of how we feel the world and our own presence. In this meditation, spend five minutes imagining that every surface you touch has the life energy known as *ki*. It can sometimes help to envision this as being something like invisible glitter.

1. Set your timer.
2. Breathing normally, imagine there is glitter—ki—that belongs everywhere, and other ki that can do harm if it is somewhere it does not belong (like viruses, for instance).
3. Consciously and deliberately share your beneficial ki with several objects—and receive their ki at the same time. These objects might include your coffee cup, a book, or a light switch.

4. As you touch each object, pause slightly to feel and see that each element is sharing life. For example, in the Japanese tea ceremony, the teacup, the teapot, and the spoon are each considered to be alive in a sense, and are cared for with respect and tenderness.

You cannot move through your day without accumulating and leaving behind this invisible glitter, this ki. Study how much more carefully you treat objects when this awareness exercise has been part of your day.

POST-MEDITATION EXERCISE

Big Sky

Lovely snowflakes,
they fall nowhere else!

—Dōgen Zenji, 13th-century Japanese Zen teacher and mystic

The Earth has observed so much more than the awakening of the Buddha. It has borne witness to every form of life, from one-celled creatures to the immense diversity of plant and animal life. The human species has unfortunately wrought great damage to this great interdependent enterprise. We face numerous extraordinary ecological crises, with global warming the worst among many.

This is exactly where meditation can help us begin and sustain a more responsible life. How can you touch the Earth today? How can you practice the tenderness of the cosmic mudra in your world?

Here's one suggestion: Make some quiet time, one minute to five minutes, and look up. See the clouds shaping and reshaping. Or the flickering stars. Breathe. Don't get busy with something else, or take out your phone for a photo. Just witness the great show of sky that is given to you exactly where you are. Stay with it as a minute or so passes. This simple act, often brings on a patience (and wonder) that is surprisingly sustaining and can refuel our work of protecting this planet and our fellow beings from harm.

TAMING THE GREAT BEAR OF PAIN

Sometimes when we sit down to meditate, our bodies may growl with discomfort. Without the distractions of daily life, we become even more aware of whatever aches—the posture we've chosen aggravates our knees or hips, and all we want to do is move away from the pain. Even though the instruction is to never sit in such a way that causes any physical harm, this growling bear of interior dialogue may insist dramatically that we'll never walk again if we don't move.

There are two important things to remember. First of all, be careful and kind as you establish your posture. Don't force old legs into a lotus position in some misguided idea that doing so will be more spiritual. Take a minute or so to get aligned and comfy as you start. When you've done this, any growly voice that emerges as you sit can be dealt with by realizing you will be fine. No one (in my 40-plus years of experience) has done any permanent damage to themselves by sitting still for a half hour. Acknowledge the bear, and let its growls go by like you would any other thought. Eventually, it will stop pushing you around.

Second, recognize that physical pain isn't something any of us get to skip in this lifetime. Shit happens, and we can't avoid pain completely in life. But we can choose what we do with our attention. If you can let the dramatic thoughts that cluster around the sensation float on down the river, you'll be a calmer, less frightened, and more resilient human being.

PRINCIPLE 3

You Are the Right One

Make no comments, complaints, criticisms, appraisals, avowals, sayings, shooting stars of thought, just flow, flow . . . *shut up, live, travel, adventure, bless, and don't be sorry.*

—Jack Kerouac

Zen is leaving the passenger seat. To practice is to stop waiting for someone else to fix our life, to tell us what to do, to affirm our direction. We stop deferring and apologizing for taking up space, and understand that this journey is up to us and the blame game is over. In the story of the Buddha, though he had deep respect for all the teachers he studied with, there was something he ultimately had to come to on his own. While he loved his family and the weave of things that supported him, they couldn't do it for him. He, and every person who will ever awaken, had to turn inward, sit down in the ground of being, and see for himself. It's not that judgment, commentary, criticism, and appraisal are useless—they just don't drive you all the way home. You have to do that for yourself. Why? Because there is no one else who can. And you alone have exactly what is required.

Your Life Is Enough

There's a critical difference between getting caught up in ego and realizing ultimate responsibility. When the Buddha was enlightened, he is believed to have said, "Between Heaven and Earth I alone am the awakened one." This wasn't a statement of rank narcissism but instead a radical inclusion: He no longer saw anyone as "outside" or "other than."

Modern Zen teacher Kōdō Sawaki Roshi makes essentially the same point: "You can't trade even a single fart with the next person. Each and every one of us has to live out his own life. Don't waste time thinking about who's most talented. The eyes don't say, 'Sure, we're lower, but we see more.' The eyebrows don't reply, 'Sure, we don't see anything, but we are higher up.' The nose can't replace the eyes, and the mouth can't replace the ears. Everything has its own identity, which is unsurpassable in the whole universe."

Forget the Self

We're the wrong gender. We're too old. We're too young. We've got too much going on. We're physically disabled. Or emotionally exhausted. Creating reasons why we can't meditate, can't practice our lives, or can't reach a place of ongoing basic peace is something we all do habitually. The truth is, we're always practicing something—whether we're dissuading ourselves of our right to be happy, or letting go of thought, or exercising our ego. What Zen meditation does is provide an option: Practice the freedom implicit in your mind, not just the program and conditioning given to you by your family and culture. The first step is to hear yourself (and others) and the story you're buying into. The degree to which we're simply walking blind, acting out our anxieties and arrogances, is the degree to which we live in confusion.

Whenever I would express doubt in myself, my teacher used to remind me that self-doubt is just as self-involved as self-aggrandizement. Both are stuck in the idea of a separate "good or bad" identity, and the only way to get unstuck was to recognize the limits of dualistic thinking. Or, as the Zen tradition would put it, "to forget the self." This involves not believing your internal chatter and repeating it as if it were the most important thing, or the absolute truth, while missing out on being actually present. In an old Zen story the student asks, "But what remains when the self is forgotten?" The teacher smiled and replied, "The ten thousand things remain!"

LEARN TO LET GO

It is like an autumn evening under a colorless expanse of silent sky. Somehow, as if for some reason that we should be able to recall, tears well uncontrollably.

—Kamo no Chōmei, Zen hermit, in *An Account of My Hut*

Perhaps there is only one lesson, and it can be both excruciating and poignant: Everything is changing. Always. Impermanence is central to the Buddhist understanding of reality, but it is also simply the experience of being human. Sometimes we hold on, wanting what is familiar, loved, and undeniably precious. The person we treasure, the place we call home, the state of health or happiness—all are subject to the reality of change. The upside of impermanence, of course, is that things we dislike or struggle with will also change. We won't always have the horrid job. The hurricane will end. And, as bad as hay fever feels, it will pass. As you meditate, a kind of spiritual patience may settle in your heart. You will find that the habit of grasping onto things will likely lessen as you practice genuinely. As you let go of passing thoughts in zazen, the ability to let tears fall and allow things to change becomes authentic. Not always easy, sometimes heartbreaking, but honest to the bone, your practice becomes simple, coherent, and as strong as the silent sky.

True Nature Doesn't Change

If your self-story is not who you are, then who are you? Taking up a meditation practice will have you bumping into this question. As you let go of passing thoughts (or more accurately, stop denying that you cannot actually hold on to anything), the river of thoughts flows through, and you no longer identify with stray bits of flotsam and jetsam. The circumstantial self-definition begins to dissipate and true nature starts to awaken. What is true nature? While the answer is different for everyone, it's helpful to note that true nature doesn't change depending on circumstances; that's what makes it true nature. Everything else we can point to—being a good person, being a creep, being an artist, being a parent—depends on circumstances.

The fundamental delusion of humanity is to suppose that I am here and you are out there.

—Hakuun Yasutani, Roshi, 1885–1973

MEDITATION

10 MINUTES

Breath by Breath

Meditation is embodied practice and, as such, it involves centering on one's breath. But why is breath a perfect meditation focus? Because it is always there—after all, if you are alive, you are breathing.

1. Set your timer, take your meditation position, and align your posture.
2. Establish your mudra and set your intention.
3. Direct your attention to your breath.
4. You don't have to remember a special phrase or repeat a mantra someone else provided you—just breathe naturally. Let your attention focus on your breath.
5. Feel your breath and notice how the lower abdomen rises with the inhale and the chest warms a little. Then observe the subtle sensation as the intake of breath turns

continued

and becomes exhale. The breath may bump into tension sometimes, and other times it won't be blocked at all. Regardless, simply follow the breath with gentle attention.

Some people find that the act of giving attention to the breath creates a temporary self-consciousness about it. For a minute or so, the breath may feel tighter, as if you're figuring it out and have somehow forgotten how to just breathe. It's like the old joke about destroying a golfer's ability to relax and swing by asking them, "Do you inhale or exhale when you begin your backswing?" Trust me: This will pass. You've been breathing all your life, and you can meditate and breathe. Go through the few moments of awkwardness, and you'll be back in your body and able to notice and focus on the breath. Over time, this will build concentration as well as a deep sense of calm.

MEDITATION

5 MINUTES

Only You Can Heal

American poet Mary Oliver wrote, "Attention is the beginning of devotion." Seldom do we recognize how our attention can profoundly change people and situations. When we listen to and really hear a friend, when we give our eyes over to really seeing another's suffering, that friend is transformed and that suffering is lessened. You have this capacity to heal and change the world around you. In fact, there are people and things that only you can help.

1. Find a piece of paper, pen, and a quiet place to write.
2. Close your eyes and center your breath.
3. List three people you care about—they can be living or dead, near or far.
4. Consider the first person on your list. Imagine for a moment the things you think have challenged them or caused them difficulty or pain. Don't try to come up with solutions for them; just feel it for a moment. Perhaps someone had long stretches of loneliness in their life or is currently

continued

dealing with chronic illness. Let yourself dwell in this compassion for a few moments.

5. When a minute or so has passed, make a small bow to this person, acknowledging them and their life, and their presence in your life and heart.

6. Do this for each of the three people on your list.

7. When you have finished, put the list of names on your altar (or a table where you can keep special things that remind you of your spiritual life), and end the exercise again with a small bow, hands palm-to-palm.

POST-MEDITATION EXERCISE

Reduce Friction

It's time to build your meditation practice into your daily routine. It can help to link your sitting practice to something else you're already doing. Just as you might put your vitamins by the coffee machine so that you see them when you make your morning pot, pair meditation with another habit you already have in place. Some of my students, for instance, have linked putting on their pajamas in the evening with going to meditate for five minutes. The already-in-place habit of getting into comfy clothing is now a trigger to meditate for a while. You may have to experiment with different things to find a link that works for you, but be persistent. Also work on reducing whatever causes "friction" and stops or delays you from keeping the commitment to meditate. Those who run gyms have studied what impacts how frequently people attend. For instance, if the gym is five miles away, the likelihood is that the person would go once a month. But if the distance is only three-and-a-half miles, likely attendance increases to five times a month. Even a little friction means greater capacity for commitment. Consider how you can likewise reduce the friction between your intention and what you do.

Today you are You,
that is truer than true.
There is no one alive
who is Youer than You.

—Dr. Seuss

PRINCIPLE 4

Rest Your Gaze

From the first, in people and in things, there is no such thing as trash.

—Sōkō Morinaga, Roshi

From the way people talk about "the new minimalism," it would be easy to think Zen was its elder version, "the old minimalism." There's an emphasis in the Zen tradition on nothing extra, just the right amount, not being greedy. Look at pictures of a monastery in Japan, and it invariably speaks of an elegant simplicity.

In the meditative practices of Zen, there is also a tendency to not add anything, but to use what is present. A good example of this is how we use the concentration on the breath rather than an elaborate mantra or intellectual teaching. As students encounter this apparent minimalism, it can be easy to fall into the idea that the problem lies in "too much stuff." An anxiety-based culling of everything in their lives can then suddenly take over—and no teddy bear, tchotchke, extra pair of pants, or annoying relationship is safe. This, however, is a misunderstanding. You don't need to streamline your life by throwing out all your accumulated trash. You simply need to appreciate each person and thing, completely. And that can take time.

Notice What You're Rejecting

How often have you heard someone describe the appearance of a person they dislike and been surprised at how physically repulsive that person sounds? Suddenly, a jawline, a haircut, or a clothing style all perfectly represent the moral failing or personal disappointment of this person through the eyes of the one doing the describing.

This deep habit, however immature we may know it to be, is part of most of our psyches. To practice meditation is to notice what happens when we make someone the "other," and tacitly decide that person does not belong or is not necessary or good. As we practice noticing, our habit of rejecting life in all its myriad forms becomes less dominant, and we're increasingly free to be kind, loving, and skillful. It is not that we aren't being discerning, only that we stop trying to pretend that we can send our trash into outer space to get rid of it—there is only this one great universe, and we're all in it together.

Embrace and Explore Contradictions

We are comforted by a rule, a truth. The problem with a rule or truth, however, is that they are not always true for everyone. We are pressed by life to live with contradictions and the fact of change. Just as it is important to establish good emotional boundaries, for example, it is equally important to live in terms of the essential intimacy of all things. In theory, this can feel like contradictory advice and seem like an obstacle. In practice, there's a different possibility that takes us out of the duality. How does this work when deciding whether to spend the holidays with a relative who is emotionally abusive, for example? How does the idea that "there is no such thing as trash" come into practice when it is time to clean up an indisputable and unhealthy mess? In Zen, we face apparent contradictions like these honestly and forthrightly. Meditation becomes a way to unplug the inner dialogue that keeps us spinning in hesitancy and ambiguity. To practice is to step up to your life, not just in one dramatic gesture but again and again. So, yes, you might not go to that holiday dinner. That discernment, however, does not dictate the rest of your life nor lock your relative into an ironclad identity. The next moment is arriving—how will you meet and practice it?

Nothing Ever Flies Away

Here's an old Zen story that might twist your nose: Once, Ma'stu and Pai-chang were walking and they saw some wild geese flying by. "What is that?" the master asked. "Wild geese," Paichang said. "Where have they gone?" the master asked. "They've flown away," Paichang said. Suddenly the master reached over and twisted Paichang's nose, laughing loudly, and said, "When have they ever flown away?!"

Perhaps what this story teaches is that nothing ever goes away, that every being is right here, necessary, present, not apart from our own bodies—but that explanation is pretty useless. We need to explore in our own heart how the truth of this story manifests in our individual lives, if we don't want the teacher to twist our nose, that is. For example, your ancestors live in your bones and breath—and that continuity can be a great strength. Your previous errors and unkindnesses aren't gone; they had consequences, and they inform your present sense of how important it is to manifest love and compassion. Your practice is here and now—in other words, it writes both the past and the future with fresh ink. The pen is in your hand: Now is the time and you are the one . . .

MEDITATION

5 MINUTES

The Resting Gaze

It can be a challenge to keep your eyes slightly open during meditation, so it's helpful to understand why that is the instruction. By keeping the eyes open, but in a resting state, you are practicing "letting the world be" without engaging with things. Just as you wouldn't put cotton in your ears to block out sound for meditation, you don't shutter your vision either. Everything is there, but rather than creating stories or inner dialogues about them, you bring your attention to your breathing.

1. Set your timer and take your position for seated meditation, whether that is in a chair, on the floor using a pillow, or in your wheelchair or bed.
2. Form your hands into the cosmic mudra, with thumbs lightly touching.
3. Become aware of your breath, continuing to breathe normally.
4. Make sure your spine is supporting you well by elongating and then relaxing it, allowing the small natural curve in your lower back.

5. Tuck your chin in without leaning your head forward, so that the tension releases from your neck.

6. Press your tongue gently against the upper palate.

7. Lower your gaze, letting it rest on the ground about two feet in front of you.

By resting your gaze in this way, the five minutes you'll spend in seated meditation is less broken off, separated from the rest of your day. Keeping your eyes slightly open in a soft gaze helps reinforce and reflect this continuity and ease with things.

MEDITATION

5 MINUTES

No Big Deal

Just stop making a big deal.

—John Daido Loori,
American Zen teacher

Many of us struggle with how to be the loving beings we know we're capable of being. We may have kind intentions, but fall into various habits that are anything but loving. We criticize others, put ourselves tacitly above or beneath them, and otherwise separate ourselves. The drama and pain that ensue are the history of the human race. Here's a short practice to begin to turn the tide.

1. Find a piece of paper, a pen, and a quiet place to write for five minutes.

2. After taking a few breaths to settle into yourself, write down the names of three people who had or have the capacity to rile you up. Personal, political, from childhood, your spouse—whoever comes to mind, write down their names. If you get riled up a lot, it may be hard to stop at three names, but for now, write down only three.

3. Consider the first person on your list. For the purposes of this exercise, don't go into the stories that support

you in feeling justifiably negative about them. Let those stories rest for now.

4. For a period of about one minute, imagine this person being kind. See them petting an animal or caring for someone they love—anything. Again, this does not mean you will forget your issues with them—it simply allows your mind to rest from its turmoil.

5. That is all. Do not consider all three names on your list, only the first one. You can repeat the process with the others at another time.

6. Put the list on your altar or special table, and make a small bow, palm-to-palm.

There are, of course, many "big deals" in terms of abuse and the need for justice. This exercise is about bringing one's own heart out of turmoil, allowing it to rest and be at peace rather than being riled and angry. From that rested, more peaceful place, we are able to go about the necessary activities that protect and preserve life.

POST-MEDITATION EXERCISE

Taking Care of Life

One of the keys to a meditative life is to stop blaming the people and things around us and turn our attention to how we can take care of life. A powerful off-the-cushion practice is to make a commitment to notice whenever we reject something. Whether it's the ottoman you stubbed your toe on or the president you disagree with, make a promise to "catch yourself thinking." Simply notice and as you do, let the energy drain out of the tirade. Feel the toe, know your disappointment over politics, but stay with your direct experience and stop shouting at the enemy. When you're not focusing your energy on what is wrong "out there," you'll be quicker to get some ice onto your hurting foot, reposition furniture so others don't hurt themselves, and move in whatever ways you can to create a more just and kind world.

When you plant lettuce, if it does not grow well, you don't blame the lettuce. You look into the reasons it is not doing well... Yet if we have problems with friends or family, we blame the other person. If we know how to take care of them, they will grow well, like lettuce. That is my experience. No blame, no reasoning, no argument, just understanding.

—Thich Nhat Hanh, Vietnamese Zen teacher

PRINCIPLE 5

You Are a Being of Compassion

From the perspective of compassion and reverence for life, to practice is to refrain from killing the mind of compassion and reverence.

—John Daido Loori, American Zen teacher

How do we balance appreciation for those who guide and inspire us with the call to be the mature, generous, independent beings we're here to be? When a meditative life calls an individual person, the whole world comes along. Every influence and impact becomes you. Still, everyone faces a challenge—we have to respect those who provide support along the way without becoming dependent. Most of us swing back and forth between two spiritual errors. Half of the time, we give our power away to the teacher or whomever inspires us, and the rest of the time we are so stubbornly independent that we miss the chance to receive. What is it to be able to give and receive freely, with compassion and reverence for life? Meditation helps us discern when to listen and receive, and when to rest in the wholeness that lacks nothing.

Do Not Kill Compassion

We are forever "killing" the open-heartedness available to us in our life and surroundings. We snark at one another, often at the drop of a hat, and there's a capacity for enormous cruelty in our inner dialogue. Zen's first precept, or rule for moral conduct, is: "Do not kill." This is taught, studied, and understood with various levels of depth and subtlety. But for beginning meditators, I emphasize not "killing" the mind of compassion. This means we have to be alert to the habitual unkindness we bring to our self and others and explore what happens when we stop being the sniper who removes every bit of tenderness from daily life. You don't have to create a saccharine dialogue to replace the mean attitude you may have been inadvertently nurturing. Just lay off the habit of firing at goodness when it shows up. If you need a hand and it is offered, that's okay. If someone falls down in front of you, help them up. If you are in a place where everything is closed down and someone opens a window of insight, take it and be grateful. Likewise, don't be stingy with your own love. In the Zen tradition, this particular "non-killing" often means a person becomes open to, and in a sense, creates, a teacher. Teachings begin to arrive, helping the shuttered heart begin to see some light, and a student comes to life.

STRESS RELIEF: TRY CHANTING OM

Chanting has a long history in Zen, and it functions in monasteries to bring a group of practitioners into greater harmony, creating one voice out of many. In home practice, some students are also helped by having a chant or several to do, particularly as they prepare to get up from seated meditation. You'll find a variety of chants useful for this purpose, but none is simpler to remember than "Om." Students of yoga will recognize this, as it is often chanted at the beginning and end of classes.

Some explanations of the practice of chanting Om are very esoteric. I once heard a yoga teacher explain that the sound Om, when chanted, vibrates at the frequency of 432 Hertz, which is the same vibrational frequency found throughout everything in nature. But to get started, it's probably most helpful to simply recognize that making a vibrational sound over and over again deeply aligns the central nervous system and is very relaxing. For this reason, Om is also handy when you need to release a little stress. If you're stressed at work, for example, try a little "Om" chanting, even if silently—you'll reap the same benefits without freaking out your coworkers.

Symbolically and physically, to chant Om is to acknowledge our connection to nature and all other living beings. It has its roots in Hinduism, where it's both a sound and a symbol rich in meaning and depth. When pronounced correctly, it sounds more like "A-U-M" and consists of four syllables: A, U, M, and the silent syllable.

The first syllable is A, pronounced as a prolonged "awe." The sound starts at the back of your throat and is stretched out. When you do this, you will feel your solar plexus and chest vibrate a little. The second syllable is U, pronounced as a prolonged "oo," and the sound gradually rolls forward along your upper palate. With this, you'll feel your throat also begin to vibrate. The third syllable is M, pronounced as a prolonged "mmmm" with lips closed and your front teeth gently touching. You'll also feel the top of your mouth very slightly vibrate. The last syllable is actually called "the deep silence of the Infinite." In other words, don't skip also feeling the silence and stillness. Let the "mmmm" stretch out into the deep silence.

Shedding Adoration

Students have flaws. Teachers have flaws. There is a whole lot of humanity going around all the time, and so to study requires being somewhat alert. One thing that tends to happen when a person begins to meditate and study their life is that whoever helped them get started becomes a wisdom figure of sorts. There can be a great deal of idealization. Whether it's a book, lecture, or one-to-one encounter, we tend to profoundly appreciate whoever helped flipped the switch in the dark. Sometimes, this translates simply into deep respect and a long path of study together. Other times, it gets warped, and the student thinks of themselves as somehow lesser and the wisdom figure as nothing but holy. Getting this warp straightened out can take some time and discernment. A teacher understands that students go through this process of putting them on a pedestal of sorts and will help by shedding any adoration coming their way. And even if they don't, most teachers will likely disappoint in either some slight or egregious way that ends the student's implicit worship. In the best cases, we develop a capacity to move into deeper study, to see what we previously couldn't, and to appreciate that someone provided a path for us to find ourselves.

Leave Your Masks Behind

We're living in a time when interactions, especially on social media, can become incredibly coarse and injurious in a flash. Too often, anonymity seems to bring out aggression. By meditating, you take up a path that is both without sentimentality and at the same time quintessentially kind. You acknowledge whatever and whoever arises: the thought, the feeling, the person. You return to the breath, the body, and this life in all its interconnectedness. As you sit in meditation, there is a holographic sense in which you are meeting every part of reality. Every time you practice seeing what is arising, not getting hooked on it, and returning to your breath, you form the capacity to live in a way that is more present and available. By not carrying forward the masks and other protections we habitually use to meet the moment, we begin to meet life in a way that is straightforward and ineffably softened, yet as strong as reality itself.

MEDITATION

10 MINUTES

Be Kind to Your Mind

For this meditation, we'll be adding an assist to concentration: counting your breath. Not, as a teacher of mine once joked, to see how many breaths you have, but simply to help yourself see whether you are concentrating. After a year or so of meditating, many people are able to let go of the counting, but it is always an option during times when concentration feels more challenging.

1. Set your timer and settle into your posture.
2. Begin connecting with your breath, returning to it as the center of your concentration. Remember, if you find yourself following some train of thought, as soon as you notice it, let go of the thought and return to your breath.
3. Link your breathing with counting: inhale, count one, exhale, count two, inhale, count three, and so on, up to the count of ten. At ten, begin the counting again at one.
4. If you become distracted, begin again at number one. So if your mind drifts and

you begin reminding yourself of the things you need to pick up at the store, acknowledge the thoughts and come back to the sensation of your breath, beginning the counting with one.

It's important not to judge the content of the thoughts or yourself and your practice. Just let go, and return to the breath. You may find that during the whole meditation period, you're counting to two and starting again—and that's okay. Or you might realize that you drifted and have counted up to 25—that's okay too. Your thoughts are not the enemy, so be kind to your mind. Just gently practice deepening your ability to concentrate.

MEDITATION

5 MINUTES

The Real Work

Another of *The Seven Thresholds of Zen* deals with our work. Regardless of how we make a living, we all exert energy in some kind of work. For some, our work is our calling, for others mere necessity, required to put food on the table and a roof overhead. And then there's everything in between. I would argue that, regardless of our jobs, there is a "real work" that all humans share. To explore this real work in spiritual practice is a daily challenge. It doesn't even depend on employment. It involves our basic understanding of what we're here on this Earth to do and be.

1. Copy or memorize the Real Work threshold chant:

   Not knowing the full
   outcome of my effort
   I will be generous, resilient,
   and creative in my service.
   I will work to benefit life
   and relieve suffering.

2. At least one day every week, recite the chant three times.

Allow your mind to question the words, as well as to dwell in the feelings that arise. What questions come up for you? What do you appreciate or disagree with as you consider the words of the chant? What does it feel like to consider your work in this light?

POST-MEDITATION EXERCISE

No Heroes, No Villains

Scan your awareness for where you may have created spiritual heroes or, conversely, figures of spiritual disappointment. Is there someone who you carry around as an ideal or as the definition of "I'll never be that way"? Wherever there's an excess of reverence, can you consider the humanity of that person and allow for a moment that they are likely also deeply flawed? Can you bring to mind the people you know have done harm and allow into your private awareness that they likely also had moments where they were generous? Usually when we do this exercise, there's a tension—we don't want the bad guy to "get loose" in such a way that we become vulnerable, nor for the hero to fall into so much ambiguity that they offer us no hope. To do this exercise requires that you be safe—don't invite harm into your life. But do allow that there may be more compassion available in your heart-mind, and it will make you stronger, not weaker. We kill compassion when we limit it. We pervert reverence when we turn it into hero worship. The ones who will help you clarify this are your teachers. Give some time and attention to seeing who they are.

PRINCIPLE 6

Integrity Happens Now

You should look into whether your present life and all the experiences arising as this life share one life or not. Nothing, not one moment and not one thing, is apart from this one life. For each thing and for each mind there is nothing but this one life.

—Dōgen Zenji, *The Whole Works* (translated by Ven. Anzan Hoshin, Roshi, and Yasuda Joshu Dainen, Roshi)

Integrity is everything. It appears in small gestures, and it changes both history and the future. When we leave integrity, no drug or pill will bring back contentment. Nothing will feel right. Yet integrity is always available the moment we turn to it and practice it. Practicing meditation is the chance to manifest truth—to be whole—but it asks that we stop pretending that there is ever a time when the person we want to deceive is "out of the room." When we cheat someone or cheat on someone, even if they don't know it immediately, the world has been touched by our deceit. Integrity starts when we stop pretending that we act in isolation, and recognize that our thoughts, words, and deeds have consequences. Meditation is a giant step into a life that is lived in coherence and honesty. It asks that we find skillful ways to enact our lives in harmony with one another, limit harm, and exude creativity and generosity. Let's explore how meditation can help when our integrity feels challenged.

No One Escapes Karma

We all lie. It is often true that the only thing that separates the average person from infamous cheaters is opportunity. Create the right situation, and almost any of us will enter into the pretense that we can lie without it being a big deal. It can seem like nothing: the small imprecisions between what would be completely honest and what would make our life a little easier with a lie. Meditation, when embraced genuinely, lets us observe the tension that comes from stepping out of integrity. So please make the critically important commitment not to turn meditation into a way of becoming numb, but instead let it allow you to authentically study yourself. All actions have the impulse to continue—that's what karma is. When we lie or otherwise do harm, that harm does have impact, for which we are responsible. The good news is that we are also capable of radical healing; it begins the moment we honestly acknowledge that responsibility.

We Lie to Ourselves

In *The Honest Truth About Dishonesty*, author Dan Ariely, a professor of psychology and behavioral economics at Duke University, tells us this:

"One percent of people will always be honest and never steal. Another one percent will always be dishonest and always try to pick your lock and steal your television. And the rest will be honest as long as the conditions are right."

Unsurprisingly, the biggest obstacle to our integrity is our seemingly endless capacity for self-justification. It's pretty easy to avoid digging deep into murky situations that provide us good returns. Most of us will find a way to reconcile the broad dichotomy between our dishonest acts and our preferred perception of them. We lie first to ourselves and then to the rest of humanity. We select what we remember and we pretend it's the whole picture. Zen practice offers a different way forward. It invites patient consideration of what forces are at play each time we are tempted to lie, cheat, or steal. It asks simply that we not rationalize a better self-image. Of course, this is anything but easy. And genuine meditation is invaluable as we take up the work.

Using Injustice as an Excuse

It often feels like we live in a veritable swamp of cheating behavior, which makes living with even the mildest integrity seem a revolutionary act. As a practitioner centers their life on awareness through meditation, an opportunity emerges. We get a chance to consider how we might set the stage to help ourselves, and other people, to be more honest.

It's helpful to spend time understanding what leads humans to be so at odds with integrity. In his book, which I often recommend to my students, Ariely examines the contradictory forces that drive us to cheat and that can also keep us honest. He points out that one significant key is to bring attention to how we react to unfairness. Does our sense of self and appropriate action change when someone treats us with less than proper respect? Ariely gives the mild example of how easy it is to work more or less hard depending on our perception of how we're being treated compared to our peers on the job. If we feel disrespected, it becomes easy to slack off without confronting the injustice. So what gets lost is our commitment to excellence and being honest with ourselves about our actions. What would happen if we trained ourselves to bring attention to our integrity when we're in the midst of an injustice?

MEDITATION

5 MINUTES

Step-by-Step

Walking meditation helps break up periods of seated meditation. It gives the knees some relief, provides a chance to use the restroom, and, most important, helps you learn to maintain a meditative mindset while the body is more stimulated through movement.

1. Following a five-minute or longer period of seated meditation, make a small seated bow and come to your feet.
2. Keeping your eyes lowered, fold your hands at your waist.
3. Know which route you will take (you only need a short hallway) and face that direction.
4. Take a breath or two, just to get your feet solidly under you.
5. As you make your next exhale, move one foot forward half the length of the other foot.

6. Inhale, and then as you exhale, move the other foot forward half the length of the first foot.

7. Continue walking very slowly like this, letting your attention settle on the sensation of your feet lifting, stepping, and landing, until you have walked down the hallway and circled back to your place.

8. Acknowledge and let go of other thoughts as they arise. When you have completed the path, end with another small bow.

Meditation practice offers the chance to practice being honest with yourself. There is no one to impress and no one who even cares whether you are actually practicing—it is you alone with your own heart. So if you are in a meditation when thoughts are coming fast and crazy, don't lie to yourself about it. Just practice that as it is. As you do walking meditation, and information begins to tap on the doors of all the senses, stay honest with yourself about whether you begin to chase a train of thought. Other times may be deadly quiet and dull, and you'll struggle to stay awake. It's all fine, but stay true to what is real.

MEDITATION

20 TO 30 MINUTES

OUT OF ALIGNMENT

It is a rare being who hits late adulthood without having done some things they feel were out of alignment with their deepest values. This is an invitation to make things right, acknowledging at the same time the things you cannot fix. For this meditation, go for a walk alone in nature or down your street.

1. Decide on where you are going to walk.
2. Set your phone or watch timer for 10 or 15 minutes so you know when to turn around.
3. Begin walking and spend your journey away from home reflecting on an instance in which you lived off-center, out of alignment with something you know in your bones to be of value. Present, past, large, small—whatever and whenever the experience of your being that is somehow untrue to yourself, let it into consciousness. This is not a time to beat yourself up. It is only about incorporating,

in the privacy of your own heart-mind, your humanity and times of forgetting who you really are.

4. At your turnaround point, take a deep breath and exhale, and turn toward home.

5. If there are clear remedial actions that you need to take around the instance you've considered, make note of them. Sometimes an apology or acknowledgment to someone is called for. Sometimes it's not.

6. Once you have noted these to yourself, just walk. Let your mind and heart go quiet. Feel the ground under your feet. The air around you. Your breath. Let go of the story of your journey, with respect and compassion for yourself and others.

POST-MEDITATION EXERCISE

No Guilt, Just Awareness

A common complaint about meditation is that it is irrelevant. You may have heard statements like "Stop staring at your navel and feed the poor," for example. Yet we all know that we can be making exterior gestures of generosity and still have it basically be all about ourselves. Walking slowly in circles in your hallway is ridiculous—unless it is actually stepping into a new way of being. So slow walking meditation is a first step. Then you leave your hallway behind and hit the streets. Pay attention to the first hour following your meditation, and make a note—actually write it down—when you seem to "lose it." No guilt, no recrimination, just begin to get a private sense of what your triggers are. We all lie. This is about getting one breath closer to being honest with yourself.

Writing a several-word reflection an hour or so after sitting creates a chance to recommit. This is as simple as making a promise: "I'd like to be in integrity today, and will keep coming back to that." Making a daily oath is helpful. Dan Ariely's work (page 90) showed that simple things take us in one direction or the other. Things that move a person toward dishonesty include having a conflict of interest or just watching others behave dishonestly. And bringing to mind an oath to be honest right before facing an opportunity to cheat helps you resist that urge. Give it a try.

PRINCIPLE 7

Living from the Inside Out

Suffering is wanting things to be other than as they are.

—Charlotte Joko Beck,
American Zen teacher

Though I would argue that Zen is actually pretty optimistic in its own ways, often people ask: "Why is Zen so pessimistic?" People mean different things when they ask this. By pessimism, they might be referring to the fact that Zen acknowledges that life can be bitter and painful—the first of the Buddha's Four Noble Truths. Or they may see pictures of people practicing meditation and they're sitting on little pillows for hours at a time. It can look boring, like a waste of time, or even depressing. Not to mention that often Zen people look to be walking around like they're lost in a daze—expressionless, seemingly without emotion. What's at play is that when we witness someone's inner struggle for liberation, there's simply not much to see—it can look pretty dismal from the outside in. It's important to appreciate that, far from being dull or pessimistic, your meditation will bring you into a fierce alignment with things as they are. That's the only real way to relieve the suffering of the spirit.

Meditation Is Anything but Dull

Part of what draws a person to meditation is that they have begun to question who they really are. We begin to entertain questions like: "Who is having this thought?" Or "Why am I here, bumping around planet Earth?" We may wonder what it is to step "outside" ourselves and see from another perspective. For some, the question of why the suffering of innocents exists—and what our responsibility is in this vast set of circumstances and mysteries—drives a meditative life.

For the person engaged in meditation, exploring the root of who they are is anything but boring. In the mind of meditation, you'll be pondering daily some of the most stimulating and engrossing subjects a person can encounter in a lifetime. To observe someone meditating is not so different from watching anyone engrossed in anything—a video game, a good book—so much that they are oblivious to everything around them. They may have a void expression or seem a bit distracted. So be aware of not prejudging that meditation will be a dull ride. You are embarking on perhaps the most important, at times daunting, often life-changing activity a person can take up. You'll be living from the inside out, trusting your own experience rather than the judgment and presumptions of others.

Embracing the Emptiness

Practitioners often get so thoroughly engaged in meditation that they not only lose track of what's going on around them, but they even lose track of themselves. In effect, the meditator kind of "disappears," entering the emptiness of being, referred to as *sunyata*. But emptiness doesn't mean that nothing is there; it just means your ego isn't the definer of all things and isn't being engaged to create a self/other idea. It can be a little scary as a meditator when we begin to slip into deeper states of mind. We're being with ourselves in a new way, and new things always take some time to settle into. It can be helpful to connect with other meditators or a teacher if you're going through a period that feels uncomfortable. Though each of us is having a solitary experience in meditation, there are guides and friends who have been on the journey and can reassure you that what you are noticing is just part of the terrain.

Another obstacle to living from our interior is that we often want what we're finding to be different somehow. We have an idea of what "depth" should be or feel like, or we're seeing things about the patterns in our brain that we just don't like. It takes patience—and a willingness to return to the process again and again—to wear down these ideas. Or even to notice that they are just that: ideas about what's real, not reality itself.

Every Kind of Weather

From stormy to gloriously sunny, it's possible to experience every available state of mind in meditation. Part of becoming a meditative person is to sign up for all the seasons and states of the human experience. This allows the development of pure awareness without the interference of our judging and evaluating mind. Dullish times will give way to awe-inspiring, ecstatic moments. And then the weather will change again. Your job is to show up. Get inside your heart of hearts, if you will, and be awake.

Hopefully, your practice will develop the same spirit as American Buddhist nun Pema Chödrön referenced when she said, "You are the sky—everything else, it's just weather."

MEDITATION

10 MINUTES

Noticing Negative Self-Speak

Zen meditation encourages a full embrace of life and the discovering of one's own potential. It invites us to the neighborhood where we can live as who we really are, instead of the isolated hero or antihero we may have pretended to be. Settling into that neighborhood involves hearing our inner dialogue, in other words, and not taking its occasional negativity too seriously.

1. Set your timer and take your seated position.
2. Center your breath and continue to breathe normally.
3. As you sit, notice gently if you have a habit of negative self-speak.
4. Don't move to correct it, but note if this is a pattern during this particular meditation period.
5. That's it for now—just notice whether this pattern is present for you.

You can't get rid of negative self-talk by willing it away. But becoming of aware of it can help dissipate the habit. During years of teaching meditation, I've been surprised at how very habitual this is for students. They beat themselves up with an uncanny vigor. Often their thoughts are not so much random, but rather a practiced repertoire of inner dislike. I encourage you to be very gentle as you bring awareness to whether this is a pattern for you as well. Do your best not to simply layer judgment upon judgment: "I'm not doing this right. Oh, look. I just did negative self-talk. I'm such a failure at this. Damn, more negative self-talk . . ." If you can just be aware, the habit will lessen a bit. And then a bit more. And the more the negative self-talk diminishes, the more room there is for every other possibility.

POST-MEDITATION EXERCISE

Observe Yourself at Work

Take your commitment to diminish negative self-talk for a walk to work. As you arrive at your desk or counter, whatever your work space is, let that be a meditation bell of sorts. Whenever you find yourself in the middle of a derogatory self-commentary, catch it before it builds into a whole catastrophe of doubt. Again, just notice. Don't get into a new pattern around how bad it is that you think negative things about your work or yourself—just notice that it is happening. The moment you notice, and that is always the key, you have an opportunity to do something different. Until you notice, you'll just keep repeating the pattern. The wonderful thing? You can notice and gradually stop beating up on that splendid, mysterious person doing their best to get some work done!

PRINCIPLE 8

Just Wash Your Bowls

A student asked Zen teacher Joshu, "I just arrived at your monastery: Please, can you give me some guidance?"
Joshu said, "Have you had breakfast yet?"
The monk said, "Yes, I have eaten."
Joshu said, "Then go wash your bowl."

—From *The Book of Serenity*, a collection of Zen teachings

In the same way that we can throw everything into the ditch, indulging in negativity as a habit, we can also operate out of a need to aggrandize ourselves. We make a big deal out of every smidgen of insight and secure ourselves with an idea of our own enlightenment. It can be easy to become self-satisfied and not even notice that there are ways we are up to our noses in excrement. In this back-and-forth between Joshu and a student, "having eaten" refers both to literally having had some oatmeal and also having attained insight. The teacher's advice? Go wash your bowl. In other words: Move on from whatever was last and be present for what is happening now. To do that requires not holding on to positive regard, or any other remnants from the last meal.

Allow the Next Thing to Arrive

In our time, we're being advised to wash our hands for what can seem like a million times a day. This new awareness that dangerous, infectious elements will travel with us from one incidental touch to the next requires a diligence and practice that feels demanding. What is the single most important thing to do as an individual to stay well and not infect others? Wash our hands. As a physical metaphor for a spiritual truth, we'd be hard-pressed to find anything more on point. The last meal, however good or bad, needs to be released, washed away, for the next to arrive fully. Joshu—one of Zen's most straightforward (and, therefore, purely poetic) teachers—taught the same thing to his new student. Are you already full? Then you won't be able to receive. Are you carrying the last encounter forward into this one? Then what you touch now will be, in a sense, polluted by what you haven't washed away. There are many such teaching dialogues in Zen history where a master is shown helping a student realize something necessary and helpful to their understanding. But while they may seem like old stories, these dialogues come to life when their lessons are realized in this body now. Are there ways in which you are carrying forward "the last meal" and need to wash your bowls?

THE BEST TIME TO MEDITATE

What is the best time to meditate? On the one hand, it is helpful to have a schedule, and many plan their meditation for either early in the morning or just before bed in the evening. On the other hand, life happens and we don't always have the luxury of a schedule. In that case, meditate when you can. I've known many students who are parents of young children and their meditation time is whenever the baby takes a nap. To the extent you can indeed organize around what is important to you, remember that it does take time to establish a life pattern. Some studies have shown that it takes 90 days for a new commitment like exercising regularly to really become part of someone's life. So the important thing is simply to find ways to get yourself to keep showing up. I've often taught my students who struggle with finding time to meditate that they need to make the commitment embarrassingly small, such as one minute. Or just to sit down for a second in their meditation space: put butt on pillow. Touch the space, even if you can't stay. Once there, you may find that you actually do have a couple of minutes. Find some very small amount of time that you can't talk yourself out of. But also look for other opportunities for meditation in your daily life. Do you have a long train ride to work, or thirty minutes after lunch before you are needed again by your responsibilities? After a while (90 days or so), sitting down to meditate will feel as natural and necessary as brushing your teeth.

Small Gestures Have Consequences

We each are essentially quite powerful—we have impact and influence beyond our imagination. We can assist, and we can also do harm. But try to teach germ theory to children, and you recognize how resistant young humans are to this! If they can't see a germ, how can they transmit a cold? Why does it matter if they touch this and then touch that? Grown-up people are really not so different. One of the basic obstacles to "wash your bowls" is to recognize that what you do actually matters, that your small gestures have significant consequences.

Another challenge is to see that you're also not so special. Every single being, in every position and station of life, brings a particular wisdom to the table. Everyone is deeply powerful. What tends to happen is that a practitioner will have some sort of breakthrough, large or small, and they will then carry it around like a badge of honor. Others will find them pretty obnoxious, since there is nothing more annoying than someone who is convinced of their own greater wisdom. But we all do this, again and again—we've "eaten" and think we can see clearly now. But if we're fortunate, a friend, teacher, or spouse will knock us off our high horse and send us to the kitchen with our dirty dish!

MEDITATION

10 MINUTES

The Jaw Jut

One telling thing that we all seem to do during insecure times, when we're feeling a kind of "proving" energy, is jut our jaw forward. It actually looks like the position of someone who might be saying, "Oh yeah? Well, prove it!" Or "I am SO okay!" You could say the bowl is full when this is happening: we've got attitude in our posture. This meditation helps us see how our inner attitude expresses itself in our physical posture and when we simply need to stop and wash our bowl.

1. Set your timer and take your meditation position.
2. Center your breath and continue to breathe normally.
3. As you establish your posture, pay particular attention to how you're situating your head. Look down and bring your eyes almost closed, letting your gaze rest about two feet in front of you.
4. Press your tongue against the upper palate lightly, letting the tip rest on the back of the front teeth.
5. Pay attention to how your inner attitude expresses itself. If you're getting sleepy or feeling down, you'll likely notice that your head begins

to lean forward a bit. This can create neck tension, so when you notice this, bring your head back to center.

6. Often when we are feeling insecure, or prideful, we jut the jaw forward. If your jaw begins to jut forward, simply tuck it back in.

Not only will centering your head help reduce the tension in your jaw and neck when you practice, but the associated attitudes will be less powerful, too.

MEDITATION

10 MINUTES

Not Me

What do you answer if someone asks who you are? If you're like most people, you give a list of aggregates and accomplishments, attributes and failures. But is that really who you are? Is the 10-year-old who lost the spelling bee, the business executive who retired, the jock or the civil rights worker the real you? What identity do you carry around, and why? The identities we're attached to often reveal themselves only when we're feeling in some way insulted: "I'm not an idiot!" Or "I'm a good person!" While the seemingly lucky among us go through life never being insulted, most people will have occasion to feel the flare of our quietly loved identities challenged. This meditation helps us deal with those moments.

1. Set your timer and sit quietly in a comfortable position where you won't be disturbed.
2. Center your breath and continue breathing normally.
3. Consider whether you've ever felt insulted.
4. What identity did it bring up for you? What idea about yourself made it uncomfortable to have challenged? If you can't remember an incident, can you imagine anything that could be said about you that would be particularly difficult?

5. Can you understand why that particular identity is important to you?

Doing this reflection won't rid anyone of their preferred identities, but it may let us feel what we hold on to a little more clearly and be more flexible as the inevitability of change and misunderstanding take place in our lives.

POST-MEDITATION EXERCISE

Don't Be a Jerk

Even if the whole universe is nothing but a bunch of jerks doing all kinds of jerk-type things, there is still liberation in simply not being a jerk.

—Eihei Dōgen (1200-1253),
translation by Zen teacher Brad Warner

We can be anything: kind, angry, self-effacing, arrogant, angels, and jerks. In the Buddhist tradition, there are "precepts" that outline some of the ways to not be jerks. In other words, to live with less self-centeredness and greater benevolence. One of these precepts is "See the Perfection—Don't Speak About Other's Errors and Faults." Another is "Realize Self and Other as One—Don't Elevate the Self and Blame Others."

As you enter your practice off the meditation pillow, let's take up these two precepts. First of all, what would your day look like if you swallowed the urge to speak of how someone else failed or what their essential faults comprised? You felt it coming up, noticed it, and just didn't give it expression. This precept doesn't mean that you don't work to eliminate harm and keep beings safe. It does mean that, just like we teach children, while certain actions may be bad or harmful, there are no bad *people*. The same wisdom holds true into adulthood, though we quite often forget it.

Second, what would your day look like if, whenever you felt like blaming someone else and elevating yourself in the process, you just noticed, inserted a breath or two, and kept quiet? Again, we're not talking about abandoning justice—just slowing down the way we separate and judge. Most folks find that when they practice these precepts for a day, that day is more likely to be touched by "Seeing the Perfection" and "Realizing Self and Other as One."

PRINCIPLE 9

Your Body Knows

Think with your whole body.

—Taisen Deshimaru, Zen priest (1914–1982)

Most of us think (or fret) about our body pretty much nonstop, even as we largely take it for granted. Do we look attractive? What about our health? We're getting older. We want to be stronger. And it would be incredibly nice if people thought we were physically impressive. A huge slice of our economy is devoted to addressing our preoccupation with our bodies. And it makes sense—who would we be without the "skin bag"? Zen asks that we consider whether there can be a self without the body and before we go too far down that road, where exactly is this self that "has" a body? Most of us tend to skip around—one minute we're looking through our body's eyes at the world, and the next we're placing our perspective outside, examining ourselves as if in a mirror. Are we just a flow of seeing, hearing, feeling, tasting, and smelling? As Zen teacher Deshimaru said, the whole body is required for even a single thought. So let's explore this great body with an open mind.

The Body Is a Beautiful Mystery

Mahayana Buddhism, of which Zen is a part, has some intriguing teachings about being a body. In part, it wants to shake up our presumptions and bring about a greater sense of what might be at work in the relationships between mind and body. There is even a provocative teaching that explores the Buddha having three bodies:

1. The *dharmakaya*, or truth body, which is all-encompassing, measureless. It is perfect and beyond perception and concept.

2. The *sambhogakaya*, or enjoyment body, which is the perceived body of perfect meditation and teaching.

3. The *nirmanakaya*, the transient historical body, which appears in our world for the purpose of teaching.

All of this is to say that the biological human body really is an incredible and unfathomably complex occurrence. Hundreds of years of medical science has really still barely scratched the surface of how it functions. We don't know exactly how the brain regulates so many things so perfectly, how it adjusts to a myriad of contingencies, creating everything from how to tie a shoelace to social systems and Shakespearean poetry. With more than

25,000 miles of blood vessels in the human body, blood flows from prebirth to death, and every organ in the body is supported. We don't know clearly what the consciousness associated with the body actually is, but it's a consciousness capable of so many things, including knowing itself.

Open Your Body

Many of my students are differently abled or elderly. They face what we will all inevitably face: the unpredictability of capacities. Their practice includes watching thoughts and feelings of betrayal and sadness arise as what once was possible becomes out of reach. Each of us have completely individual paths through the physical. Some have abilities or characteristics that society makes accommodation for, whether it be a "normal" height, weight, mobility, and so on. The one certainty is that these things will change. We bend over with age, don't run like we used to, don't fit into the airline seat, or, for any number of reasons have chronic pain or suddenly can't walk. There is no way to secure your fortune in this. And we also become aware of challenges that others may have faced their entire lives: countertops at the wrong height, entryways with steps, bathrooms that are inaccessible. We are vulnerable beings of all shapes, ages, sizes, and abilities. There is an invitation in our practice to see both the wondrous mystery of being physical and our present and incipient vulnerabilities. For most, the primary obstacle will be not breathing in that vulnerability, but instead letting it soften our hearts and minds, bringing a deeper genuineness to practice. What would it take to be open to your body as the practice of your life itself?

Not Difficult, Not Easy

Layman Pang (740–808) said, "Difficult, difficult, difficult. Like trying to scatter ten measures of sesame seed all over a tree." Hearing this, his wife, Laywoman Pang, said, "Easy, easy, easy. Just like touching your feet to the ground when you get out of bed." Their daughter, the wise Lingzhao, responded, "Neither difficult nor easy. On the hundred grass tips, the ancestors' meaning."

As we take up the physical aspects of practice, we'll face our personal histories and personalities. If you're a person who "lives in your head," then paying attention to the seemingly obsessive instructions on posture may be a point of rebellion. If you're a person who is very focused on being physically adept, the rebellion may be more around stillness. The great talkers among us resist the silence, and the quiet ones want to say no when it is time to speak. To commit to a practice that is embodied is to reckon with all this—the rebellions and resistances that live in the body will let themselves be known. Sometimes the truth of it will be "difficult, difficult, difficult," as the layman Pang said. This meditative life will seem impossible and, frankly, unreasonable. Other times it will be as unprovoking and undemanding as letting your feet hit the ground while getting out of bed. Easy-peasy. What was all the fuss about anyway? The wisdom of Lingzhao, whose observations are usually the most insightful in these ancient household teaching dramas, will resonate in our cells. She points to what happens when we're not basing our practice on the dichotomy of easy and difficult. The "ancestors' meaning," the nondual truth of body and mind, then sparkles from every grass tip.

MEDITATION

1 TO 3 MINUTES

Alternate Nostril Breathing

This meditation to calm the central nervous system can be done anywhere and is very helpful in times of stress or anxiety. If you're in a situation where you feel riled up, this provides a quick way to come back to a calmer state, where you can interact with greater ease.

1. Wash your hands.
2. Set your timer and take your seated meditation position. If you're at work or in a difficult social situation, you can use a bathroom stall for just a few minutes as a quasi-private mini-temple to do this practice.
3. Keep your breath slow, smooth, and continuous. You should be able to breathe easily throughout the practice.
4. Place your left hand on your left knee, and lift your right hand up toward your nose.
5. Exhale completely and then use your right thumb to close your right nostril.

continued

6. Inhale through your left nostril and then close the left nostril with your pinkie and ring fingers.

7. Open the right nostril by lifting your thumb and exhale through this side.

8. Inhale through the right nostril and then close this nostril.

9. Open the left nostril by lifting your fingers and exhale through the left side. This is one cycle.

10. Continue for up to 3 minutes and always complete the practice by finishing with an exhale on the left side.

11. Wash your hands again.

You may be familiar with this technique from yoga. In Sanskrit, it's known as *nadi shodhana pranayama*, which translates as "subtle energy clearing breathing technique."

MEDITATION

1 TO 3 MINUTES

Capacity During Incapacity

This is a meditation for when you are ill or incapacitated. Everyone knows how frightening it can be to not be able to do what we're used to doing. When we're laid low with a high fever, or wracked with coughs or stomach distress, it can seem like a betrayal—or that we simply cannot bear what is happening. Even though we are aware from an early age that everyone will die, and that life involves physical illness, when it is our immediate experience it is still somehow shocking. Your meditation practice can also take place during these times and help with some of the fear and distress.

1. Set a timer.
2. Center your breath and continue to breathe as normally as possible.
3. As much as you are able, take the time to be reflective.
4. Notice whether you are repeating any particular fear statements to yourself.
5. Imagine briefly those statements dissipating. This isn't about whether they are true or false, just that you don't need them to live the truth of what you're experiencing. And they may be making you a little less resilient.

continued

6. Take another brief moment to recognize any care or support you're being given. If you have a bed to rest in, care from another, privacy to heal, food, medicine, sunshine—anything. Again, don't make a demanding assignment of this, just touch it with your mind. Simply feeling it can give you strength.

7. Remember that you have a habit of recovering. Everything you've ever been sickened with in the past, you have survived. That's a strong record.

8. Now, just rest . . .

POST-MEDITATION EXERCISE

Trust the Wisdom of the Body

My dharma grandfather, and one of my teachers over several decades, was Maezumi Roshi. Like most teachers, he would repeat certain things again and again. The words most associated with Maezumi were: "Trust yourself." He was known for this, and it helped many, many students. In response to the most intricate question, he might simply lean forward and say in his Japanese accent, "Aahh . . . please just trust self. Not about me, not about Buddhism, just trust now. Yes?"

Maezumi Roshi was also known to struggle with alcoholism, and the communities where he taught experienced a great deal of pain that grew out of his drinking. I remember asking him years ago as a young student why this was such a difficult thing—why couldn't his practice help him not to drink? He eventually had to engage rehab to find a way to stop, and grieved for years the harm he had caused a great number of people. I tell this story because he would want me to, and because it is important to recognize that sometimes we need to do other kinds of work as well as meditation. Study your life and see if there are patterns of harm you are creating, no matter how deeply or often you meditate. Have others let you know that you have hurt them? Consider seriously that your body may be asking you to bring into your life people who can help you and who have the skills to help you understand why it is difficult to untangle on your own. This is the deeper meaning of "trust yourself"—and listening to it can make for a much more loving world.

PRINCIPLE 10

Contentment amid Chaos

No mud, no lotus.

—Thich Nhat Hanh, Vietnamese Zen teacher

The blossom of the lotus is extraordinary. In many Eastern cultures, it is considered not only the most beautiful of all flowers but also a symbol of transformation. This is because it looks pristine but thrives only in the muddiest of swamps. It requires the least desired elements—the muck, mire, and fires of confusion—to create blossoms that are perfection itself. In this way, the lotus is regarded as a kind of teaching on how each of us can encounter and transform the things we reject about our individual lives or the often-chaotic world. In fact, the great news of Buddhism is that the things we find most difficult—the obstacles and chaos—provide exactly what is needed for our peace of mind and compassionate activity.

The Problem Is Not the Problem

Most of us have a picture in our mind of what true contentment would look like. In this scenario, the voices of sadness, loss, loneliness, illness, dying, and death have been calmed. Gone are the overlapping, overwhelming crises of the day. Gone is the sense of being inadequate to the suffering within and around us. We are sufficient, at ease, and open to the moment. The one thing we all usually get wrong is that we think the key to reaching this place of contentment comes from getting whatever it is we sense is missing. If we only had enough money, better health, a saner world, sweeter relationships or (fill in the blank here), then we could be not only content but quite happy.

The problem is that this thought pattern is actually upside down. While it is true that having food, shelter, and medical care make for a better life, even those with the fortune of stability in these areas quite often are still full of distress. What "no mud, no lotus" asks is that we realize that the mud is not the issue. Or to put it another way, the problem is not the problem—separation is. The more you try to get rid of the problem, deny it, or bargain with it, the more your suffering arises and continues. This is the dis-ease the Buddha spoke of as dukkha in the Four Noble Truths, his first teaching (page 7). He taught that relief of dukkha depends first on letting go of the idea that a condition "should not be." If you hold on to that idea, you are not only blocking yourself from true honesty, but also from the contentment that is available when you stop swatting away what is real.

Allow the Lotus to Bloom

The first thing that blocks our contentment is the thought that something else is needed before it can be present. Usually, the opposite is true: There is something extra, not something missing. That "extra" is the thoughts we keep adding to the brew, that "it shouldn't be like this" or "this is too hard." If only we could be given a different spiritual challenge, then everything would be just fine...

So the real challenge is to first accept that our lives are not lacking anything—we don't need something or someone else to make it perfect. This very circumstance is exactly what is needed for the lotus to bloom. We have the perfect muddy waters to embrace a contented, awakened life.

Notice Your Habitual Train

When your health, relationships, or the world itself goes out of balance, it can seem like there is no alternative than to reject what is present. There are hundreds of ways—some quite creative and some temporarily effective—that we all attempt to reject reality. But contentment ultimately comes from only one thing: trust. Contentment doesn't mean complacency. It's actually what makes available the fierce, intelligent, compassionate energy that is our birthright. What does this look like?

Let's say you hear a disturbing report on the news. There has been some great cruelty, or an environmental disaster that is ongoing, or news about a pandemic that is overwhelming. Step one is to acknowledge the natural next thoughts. Just notice. You may jump on the "blame train." Or the "hopelessness train." And, especially in the age of modern media, many ride the "train of distraction" for miles and miles without any awareness. So, notice, breath by breath, your state of mind and the habitual trains you ride.

Then focus. You're going to get off the train. You're going to trust yourself enough to be real. This takes quiet courage, and you have what it takes.

Let the situation in, and let yourself dwell right where you are, without adding anything. Just like in seated meditation, this is a very intimate way of being. Instead of indulging thoughts about the situation, you simply stop separating yourself from it. Don't turn away, deny, or pretend. Just breathe it in, and without falling into any story, meaning, or solution, stay present. As soon as you catch yourself involved in a story, come home again to your breath. This may take some time, as thoughts, emotions, and ideas rush in. Eventually the train of reactive thoughts will slow down.

MEDITATION

25 TO 30 MINUTES

Being the Waves

In this meditation, we'll sit a little longer to go through several of the waves that are common to meditating during a crisis or great challenge. I'd like for you to experience staying with the meditation as these changes happen.

1. Set a timer for this longer period and decide that, whatever your experience, you won't leave the meditation until it rings.
2. After establishing your intention and posture, begin your meditation.
3. Connect with and count your breath up to ten, returning to one whenever you reach the count of ten or find you've become distracted.

At the beginning of your sitting period you'll be settling physically and mentally. During crisis periods, anxious thoughts may come in a veritable rush, and physical discomfort may be more present. Work with whatever arises, acknowledging and not judging.

The period will be valuable even if your thoughts never fully quiet down. Do your very best not to fidget, but to deepen into your body by being still. People often find that when they let the stillness sink into their bones, after what seems a short while, the timer will go off.

MEDITATION

5 MINUTES

Do One Thing

During great challenges, we all tend to look at the overwhelming aspects and become intimidated. Your Zen practice slows down that process, giving you a chance to focus your energy on what's right in front of you rather than the oceans of problems and possibilities your mind wants to busy itself with. You may not, for instance, be able to establish a stockpile of food and medicine that will get your family through years of pandemic-level crises and infrastructure breakdown. But you can make your partner a cup of tea. You can do one thing. And then you can do another. And then another.

1. Set a timer and take up your meditation position.
2. Center your breath and continue to breathe normally.
3. Meditate for five minutes.
4. Before you get up from your five-minute meditation period, bring one thing to mind that you can do that will serve another being—something straightforward, like feeding the dog, making a cup of tea, or calling your mom.
5. Go do that one thing.

As the day goes on, periodically reflect on what you could do at that moment to make life just a little better for someone somewhere. And then go do that thing.

POST-MEDITATION EXERCISE

Feed the Lotus

In Zen, when we take up our lives in this way, the chaos and crises around us deepen our practice. As we practice not standing apart from things, in judgment or fear, a profound and deep calm becomes available. From that calm, whatever action is appropriate arises naturally. Rest or exercise. Attention or action. Medicine or acceptance. It is natural, of course, to become afraid in crises because we love and value life, and don't want to lose this life, or have those we know and love suffer or lose theirs. Yet there is a path through these times that we also intuitively sense—it arrives at our feet when we access the underlying love and value of all beings, and let that move us. When confusion and fear swirl around your life, remember that you are one of the lucky people on this Earth. You have encountered the meditative path, have a sense of your inner resources, and the "mud and fire" challenges will only feed the lotus of your compassionate mind. May we realize the awakened way together!

RESOURCES

BOOKS

Zen Meditation in Plain English by John Buksbazen

An excellent, practical introduction to Zen meditation. Written in a warm, easily accessible style, this book appeals to anyone with an interest in meditation, Zen, Buddhism more widely. The book emphasizes the importance of receiving good instruction and finding groups to practice with while laying out the necessary steps to practice Zen meditation on your own.

Zen Mind, Beginner's Mind by Shunryu Suzuki

In the thirty years since its original publication, this book has become one of the great modern Zen classics. It's a book to come back to time and again as an inspiration to practice.

Zen Women: Beyond Tea Ladies, Iron Maidens, and Macho Masters by Grace Schireson

This landmark presentation at last makes heard the voices of women in Zen. Through exploring the teachings and history of these largely overlooked ancestors, it presents a more gender-balanced picture of Dharma practice.

The World Could Be Otherwise: Imagination and the Bodhisattva Path by Norman Fischer

An inspiring reframe of classic Buddhist teachings, Zen teacher Norman Fischer writes that the paramitas, or "six perfections"—generosity, ethical conduct, patience, joyful effort, meditation, and understanding—can help us reconfigure the world we live in.

Waking Up to What You Do and *A Zen Practice for Meeting Every Situation with Intelligence and Compassion* by Diane Eshin Rizzetto

These books use the Zen precepts as tools to develop a keen awareness of the motivations behind every aspect of our behavior from moment to moment.

WEBSITES

Buddhist Temple of Toledo (OH), buddhisttempleoftoledo.org
Hermitage Heart Zen (NC), hermitageheartzenbmt.com
San Francisco Zen Center (CA), sfzc.org
Soto Zen Buddhist Association, szba.org
Women in Zen, zenwomen.com
Zen Mountain Monastery (NY), zmm.org

INDEX

A

Account of My Hut, An (Chōmei), 55
Adoration shedding, 80
Altars, 16–17
Alternate Nostril Breathing
meditation, 127–128
Ariely, Dan, 90–91
Awareness, 31–32, 96

B

Be Kind to Your Mind meditation, 82–83
Beck, Charlotte Joko, 99
Being the Waves meditation, 138–139
Big Sky exercise, 48
Body, 122–126
Body positions, 18–21
Book of Serenity, The, 109
Breath by Breath meditation, 57–58
Breathing, 22, 31–32, 57–58, 127–128
Buddhadasa Bhikkhu, 39
Burmese position, 19

C

Capacity During Incapacity
meditation, 129–130
Chanting, 78–79
Chödrön, Pema, 103
Chōmei, Kamo no, 55
Compassion, 75–77
Contentment, 134–137
Contradictions, 66
Cosmic mudra, 21, 43–45

D

Daystart meditation, 34–35
Deshimaru, Taisen, 121, 122
Discomfort, 41–42, 49, 136–139
Distractions, 12
Do One Thing meditation, 140
Dōgen Zenji, 87. *See also*
Eihei Dōgen
Don't Be a Jerk exercise, 118–119
Dukkha (suffering), 7–8, 135

E

Earth, 39–41
Eightfold Path, 9–10
Eihei Dōgen, 118. *See also* Dōgen Zenji
Embodying Kindness
meditation, 44–45
Enlightenment, 6

F

Feed the Lotus exercise, 141
Four Noble Truths, 6–8, 135
Full lotus position, 19

G

"Geographic cure," 41

H

Half lotus position, 19
Handle with Care meditation, 46–47
Hanh, Thich Nhat, 72, 133
***Honest Truth About Dishonesty, The* (Ariely), 90**
Honesty, 90–91, 93

I

Identity, 52–54, 56, 116–117
Illness, 129–130
Impermanence, 55
Injustice, 91
Integrity, 88–91
Intentions, 24
Interruptions, 12

J

Jaw Jut meditation, 114–115

K

***Karma*, 29, 89**
Kerouac, Jack, 51
***Ki* (life force), 22, 46–47**

L

Letting go, 55–56
Lingzhao, 126
Loori, John Daido, 70, 75
Lotus metaphor, 134–136, 141
Lying, 89–90

M

Maezumi Roshi, 131
Mahayana Buddhism, 123
Masks, 81
Meditations. *See also* Post-meditation exercises
Alternate Nostril Breathing, 127–128
Be Kind to Your Mind, 82–83
Being the Waves, 138–139
Breath by Breath, 57–58
Capacity During Incapacity, 129–130
Daystart, 34–35
Do One Thing, 140
Embodying Kindness, 44–45
Handle with Care, 46–47

Meditations (*continued*)
Jaw Jut, 114–115
No Big Deal, 70–71
Not Me, 116–117
Noticing Negative Self-Speak, 104–105
Only You Can Heal, 59–60
Out of Alignment, 94–95
Real Work, 84
Resting Gaze, 68–69
Step-by-Step, 92–93
Water Blessing, 36
Minimalism, 64
Morinaga, Sōkō, 63
***Mudras* (hand positions), 21, 40, 43–45**
Mumon, ix, 23

N

Next thing, 110–111, 113, 140
No Big Deal meditation, 70–71
No Guilt, Just Awareness exercise, 96
No Heroes, No Villains exercise, 85
"Noble environment," 40–43
Nondualism, 3–4
Not Me meditation, 116–117
Noticing, 65
Noticing Negative Self-Speak meditation, 104–105

O

Observe Yourself at Work exercise, 106
Okumura, Shohaku, 27
Oliver, Mary, 59
"Om" chanting, 78–79
Only You Can Heal meditation, 59–60
Out of Alignment meditation, 94–95

P

Pain, 49
Pang, Layman, 125–126
Pessimism, 100
Pillows, 18
Post-meditation exercises
Big Sky, 48
Don't Be a Jerk, 118–119
Feed the Lotus, 141
No Guilt, Just Awareness, 96
No Heroes, No Villains, 85
Observe Yourself at Work, 106
Reduce Friction, 61
Taking Care of Life, 72
Trust the Wisdom of the Body, 131
Whole Works, 37
Present moment, 27–30

R

Real Work meditation, 84
Reality, 81, 136–137
Reduce Friction exercise, 61
Resting Gaze meditation, 68–69
Rogers, Will, 30

S

Sawaki, Kōdō, 53
Seiza bench, 20
Self, 53–54, 56
Self-talk, 104–106
Seuss, Dr., 61
Seven Thresholds of Zen, The, 36, 84
Siddhartha Guatama, 4–6
States of mind, 100–103
Staying put, 41–42
Step-by-Step meditation, 92–93
Suffering (*dukkha*), 7–8, 135
Sunyata (emptiness of being), 102

T

Taking Care of Life exercise, 72
Transitions, 37
Trust the Wisdom of the Body exercise, 131

V

"Verse of the Buddha's Robe," 37

W

Water Blessing meditation, 36
Whole Works exercise, 37
Whole Works, The (Dōgen), 87

Y

Yasutani, Hakuun, 56

Z

Zabuton (pillow), 18
Zafu (pillow), 18
Zazen, 15–16
Zen meditation, 3–4. *See also* Meditations
- in daily life, 11
- interior aspects of, 100–103
- knowing if you are "in," 33
- mind preparation, 23–24
- positions, 18–21
- space preparation, 16–17
- time and, 13–14, 112

ACKNOWLEDGMENTS

To Mom, who would get up at 5 a.m. to have a private, meditative cup of tea absolutely every day. The quiet she had inside herself and the ready-for-a-joke spark in her eye—these were the legacies she created. She showed me the heart of it all and winked.

To Dr. Haulk, whose lecture on the whiteness of the whale took the borders off my mind on a Tuesday. Who then joined me and a gang of poetry students for a beer and leaned over and whispered that I should lighten up, that the "biggest deal is no big deal." He showed how teaching could snap a person out of personal drama, point to the biggest reality, and be the kindest thing ever.

And to Daido Loori, Roshi, another teacher of no-big-deal, who made a monastery for thousands of us to encounter Zen dawn-to-dark, creating what he called an "archive of sanity" from a motley crew of very human beings. Words will never reach the depth of gratitude that lives in my cells.